THE COMPLETE
IDIOT'S
GUIDE® TO

Getting
Organized

FAST-TRACK

by Cynthia Ewer

ALPHA

A member of Penguin Group (USA) Inc.

For Helen Betty Townley

ALPHA BOOKS

Published by Penguin Group (USA) Inc.

Penguin Group (USA) Inc., 375 Hudson Street, New York, New York 10014, USA • Penguin Group (Canada), 90 Eglinton Avenue East, Suite 700, Toronto, Ontario M4P 2Y3, Canada (a division of Pearson Penguin Canada Inc.) • Penguin Books Ltd., 80 Strand, London WC2R 0RL, England • Penguin Ireland, 25 St. Stephen's Green, Dublin 2, Ireland (a division of Penguin Books Ltd.) • Penguin Group (Australia), 250 Camberwell Road, Camberwell, Victoria 3124, Australia (a division of Pearson Australia Group Pty. Ltd.) • Penguin Books India Pvt. Ltd., 11 Community Centre, Panchsheel Park, New Delhi—110 017, India • Penguin Group (NZ), 67 Apollo Drive, Rosedale, North Shore, Auckland 1311, New Zealand (a division of Pearson New Zealand Ltd.) • Penguin Books (South Africa) (Pty.) Ltd., 24 Sturdee Avenue, Rosebank, Johannesburg 2196, South Africa • Penguin Books Ltd., Registered Offices: 80 Strand, London WC2R 0RL, England

Copyright © 2012 by Cynthia Ewer

International Standard Book Number: 978-1-61564-231-1
Library of Congress Catalog Card Number: 2012939813

14   13   12   8   7   6   5   4   3   2   1

Interpretation of the printing code: The rightmost number of the first series of numbers is the year of the book's printing; the rightmost number of the second series of numbers is the number of the book's printing. For example, a printing code of 12-1 shows that the first printing occurred in 2012.

Printed in the United States of America

Note: This publication contains the opinions and ideas of its author. It is intended to provide helpful and informative material on the subject matter covered. It is sold with the understanding that the author and publisher are not engaged in rendering professional services in the book. If the reader requires personal assistance or advice, a competent professional should be consulted.

The author and publisher specifically disclaim any responsibility for any liability, loss, or risk, personal or otherwise, which is incurred as a consequence, directly or indirectly, of the use and application of any of the contents of this book.

Most Alpha books are available at special quantity discounts for bulk purchases for sales promotions, premiums, fund-raising, or educational use. Special books, or book excerpts, can also be created to fit specific needs. For details, write: Special Markets, Alpha Books, 375 Hudson Street, New York, NY 10014.

Publisher: *Mike Sanders*

Executive Managing Editor: *Billy Fields*

Executive Acquisitions Editor: *Lori Cates Hand*

Development Editor: *Susan Zingraf*

Senior Production Editor: *Kayla Dugger*

Copy Editor: *Krista Hansing Editorial Services, Inc.*

Cover Designer: *Kurt Owens*

Book Designers: *William Thomas, Rebecca Batchelor*

Indexer: *Johnna VanHoose Dinse*

Layout: *Ayanna Lacey*

Proofreader: *John Etchison*

Contents

Introduction

"I've got to get organized!"

Does that statement sound familiar? Take heart—you're not alone. In recent years, the world has exploded around us. We have more stuff and less time, multitasking is the new normal, and always-on communications lengthen our day and multiply our responsibilities. In a world where VHS tapes share shelf space with DVDs and Blu-ray discs, most of us scamper to keep on top of our stuff, our space, and our time.

This book is designed to help you get organized fast. Focused on building the core elements of an organized life, it will help you find your own path to better home and personal organization. You'll get a quick grip on the skills you need for successful self-change, then use them to set goals and overcome obstacles as you get organized.

You'll learn how to cut clutter and keep it from coming back, how to build routines to speed everyday activities, how to bring order to your spaces, and how to manage time. Finally, this book will help you take aim at household paper, get organized in the workplace, and teach you what to do when you go off the rails.

How This Book Is Organized

To set the stage, **Chapters 1 and 2** zero in on what "organized" is and what it isn't, lay out the core components of an organized life, and map out your first steps on the road.

Chapters 3 and 4 take aim on clutter. You'll learn a simple method to blast through clutter decisions, craft a plan to cut clutter house-wide, and review strategies to prevent it from coming back.

Habits, routines, and activity centers take center stage in **Chapters 5 and 6.** You'll get up-to-speed with these household wonder workers and learn to put them in place to streamline every aspect of life at home.

Chapters 7 and 8 bring order to spaces around the house. You'll learn how to assign household real estate and how to create activity centers room by room for an organized home.

Time and money come into focus in **Chapters 9 and 10.** You'll tune up time-management skills with calendar and to-do lists, create a home office activity center, and establish filing and paper-handling routines to bring order to your financial life.

In **Chapter 11,** you'll take your new organizational skills to the workplace, learning how to handle different organizing styles, control workplace clutter, and build organized spaces and routines to support you throughout the workday.

Chapter 12 covers bumps you'll encounter in the road—those special challenges that throw you off the rails. You'll learn ways to bring the family on board, cope with a move, celebrate the holidays, and survive crisis cleaning. Finally, you'll learn how to reclaim your organized life quickly when you fall behind.

Extras

Beyond the chapters, this book has two appendixes that provide organizing resources and a 10-step organizing plan. You'll also find the following sidebars throughout the book—brief bright ideas that point out shortcuts and cautions along the way.

SPEEDY SOLUTION

These sidebars provide quick tricks designed to boost your organizational prowess in record time.

ROAD HAZARD

These sidebars point out hidden dangers that could slow your progress to an organized life.

Acknowledgments

Many thanks to agent Marilyn Allen, whose sharp eye and expert matchmaking led to a new partnership with Alpha Books, and to editor Lori Hand, whose enthusiasm and warmth made the writing process a pleasure. On the home front, housekeeper Denise Older kept life on an even keel; her expert collaboration on efficient home-management methods was invaluable to this book.

As always, there would be no book without the support and enthusiasm of my husband, Dr. Stephen Ewer, who lives with a writer and makes it look easy! Finally, I am deeply grateful to my grandmother, Helen Betty Townley, for a lifetime of home-making inspiration and an ocean of tender love. You're my muse, Mamma!

Trademarks

All terms mentioned in this book that are known to be or are suspected of being trademarks or service marks have been appropriately capitalized. Alpha Books and Penguin Group (USA) Inc. cannot attest to the accuracy of this information. Use of a term in this book should not be regarded as affecting the validity of any trademark or service mark.

The Fast Track to an Organized Life

Getting organized is a journey, not a destination. As with any kind of trip, to get there quickly you need to know where you're starting and where you want to go.

This chapter puts you on the fast track to organization by helping you sort out what it *means* to get organized. In the pages to come, you'll get acquainted with the basic components of an organized life and begin the process of getting organized—fast.

With a good idea of your destination, you'll be ready to pick a starting point and set up a command center for support. Ready? Let's get organized!

What Is Organized, Anyway?

Most of us have no trouble defining what it means to be *disorganized* because the evidence is all around us. When it's hard to get out the door on time because necessary household items such as car keys, handbags, or children's homework are nowhere to be found, or when bills go unpaid because they're mislaid or lost, it spells disorganization.

Understanding what it means to be organized, on the other hand, can be a bit more difficult. In a nutshell, you picked up this book because you want life to be easier. That desire to live more simply, directly, and freely is at the heart of what you mean when you say you need to get organized.

Depending on the individual, the process of getting organized may involve clearing clutter, getting control of time, revamping storage, establishing new routines, or all of these things. The precise mix varies from person to person. Someone with a clutter problem will take a different road to organization than a person who needs to improve time-management skills. The secret to getting organized fast is focusing on your own challenges, abilities, and goals, and creating your own unique path to an organized life.

What will it take to move you from where you are to where you want to be? To clear the way forward, let's examine some myths and misconceptions about the organizing process.

 SPEEDY SOLUTION

For a quick start to a more organized life, carry a small notepad with you at all times. Each time you remember an item you need to buy or a task you need to do, make a note of it. Using a notepad or smartphone to track fleeting must-do items saves time and frees your brain for more important work. Trap them now to tap them later!

Organizing Myths and Misconceptions

Sometimes efforts to get organized can get hung up on inaccurate ideas of what organization is and how you achieve it. See how many of these statements about organization you agree with:

- Getting organized takes a lot of time.
- You have to buy stuff to get organized.

- Organized homes are neat and tidy.
- Organizing systems are really complicated.

Surprise! None of these statements is true. All of them express commonly held misconceptions about the process of getting organized.

Does it take time to get organized? Sure it does, but a lot less than the time you spend fighting the day-to-day effects of disorganization.

Getting organized is like riding a bicycle. When you're just learning to ride a two-wheeler, you have plenty of false starts and stops, and you wobble a lot. But soon enough, you find your balance. From that point on, all it takes to go is a tiny push on the pedal.

Yes, you'll invest some time in the beginning stages of getting organized. But just as with that bicycle, your efforts will move you along far more quickly than they did before. Once past the first part of the learning curve, an organized life takes very little time to maintain.

What about expense? Well, who doesn't love visiting a store devoted to organizing products? Wandering down the aisles, it's easy to imagine living a serene and organized life. But oh, the price tag! Specialty organizers can carry a hefty price tag, so you decide that you can't afford to get organized—not this pay period, anyway.

Nonsense! While organizing products offer clever and useful solutions to many common problems, buying them is not a pre-requisite to getting organized. Their place in the organization process comes after the hard work has been done of cutting clutter, evaluating household storage, and making educated decisions about the requirements of your space and your stuff. None of these activities costs a dime, and neither does getting organized.

Can you tell an organized space by the way it looks? Be careful—*organized* is not a decorating style. Despite the efforts of home magazines to convince you otherwise, there's no such thing as an organized housing style.

A minimalist home can look great on the surface but dissolve into chaos when you open a drawer or search for a filed paper. On the other hand, a cozy country house, complete with scattered belongings and children's toys, can be a beautifully organized home that supports the daily life of the family that lives there. Know an organized space by the way it works, not by the way it looks.

What about all those complex organization systems out there, the ones with mission statements and planner pages and checklists? Yes, they do exist, and for many people they represent an effective path to organized living. However, structured get-organized systems are not the only route to the goal. By all means, make use of them if they work well with your organizing style, your goals, and your budget. But if all those little check boxes make your skin crawl, take heart! You can achieve the same results with nothing more complicated than a simple spiral notebook and a pen.

One Right Way—Yours

Another factor can trip you up when reaching for better home and personal organization: the guru. Browsing the bookstore or surfing online, you can encounter testimonials about this method or that writer or workshop, and all of them are glowing. "Gee," you say to yourself, "if it works for them, it has to work for me!"

If you're lucky enough to hook up with a method that meets your personal organizing needs and preferences, it'll be a match! But problems arise when you try to shove your square peg into their round hole. Experiencing setbacks when everyone around you appears to be making great strides forward can throw you off the path altogether.

The fastest way to create an organized life that you can live with is to know yourself. Your goals, your strengths, and your challenges all affect where you'll start and how you'll travel down the path.

This book helps you determine your own clutter tolerance, filing preferences, time-management style, and taste in routines to help you craft a custom get-organized plan that will work for you—and work quickly.

 ROAD HAZARD

When you're fed up with a disorganized life, it's tempting to go on the organizing equivalent of a crash diet, changing everything in your life at once. Resist the urge! Just as with weight loss, the secret to organized success is slow, steady progress. Save your energy for the long haul so you can sustain the journey to an organized life.

Components of an Organized Life

Getting organized means different things to different people. Some folks hope to be more productive. Others want help with their clutter, and still others are looking for ideas about how to run their households more efficiently.

Meet the "core four"—the essential components of an organized life:

- Controlled clutter
- Robust routines
- Organized spaces
- Well-managed time

These four elements of an organized life work together like highly synchronized acrobats. Each component contributes directly to the others; together they make up an interlaced set of skills, habits, and tools for effective living.

Looking at these components in our own lives, each of us brings a different mix of strengths to the table. One person may have a well-developed sense of time yet live a life burdened by clutter. Another, a neat freak, may have a cleaning schedule that would rival an executive housekeeper's yet never manage to make it to appointments on time.

That's why each of us will have a slightly different definition of what it means to get organized. The final goal is the same, but the specific steps any of us will take are dictated by our individual strengths and shortfalls in these four areas.

To get organized fast, we'll bolster the components that need strengthening while drawing on the power of those that currently serve us well. The goal is to create a well-balanced, flexible set of skills to carry out and support our organized life.

Controlled Clutter

Clutter is an inescapable aspect of modern life. Simply put, we are surrounded by stuff! The ability to manage and control the physical items in our environment is a baseline requirement for an organized life.

Clutter is the sand that gums up the smooth workings of day-to-day existence, and it has a direct impact on the other components of an organized life. Clutter affects your use of time; for instance, if you misplace the keys, you'll be late to the meeting. It multiplies the effort needed to clean and maintain your surroundings. It prevents you from enjoying the peace and order of your own home.

Bringing clutter under control, and instituting new mechanisms to keep it that way, is a threshold step to getting organized. This book shows you how to identify clutter, send it on its way, and keep it from coming back to haunt you.

ROAD HAZARD

Is more space the answer to the problem of clutter? It's the nature of clutter to expand to fill the area around it, no matter how spacious. Fix the underlying problem by strengthening your clutter-cutting skills, not by giving clutter a new and larger place to live in.

Robust Routines

Think of routines as the freeways on the road to organization. By grouping and streamlining a set of actions and then making their performance a habit, routines shortcut the time and effort necessary to carry out the work of your life.

Just imagine if you had to wake up each morning and make a specific decision to carry out each action of the day. You'd have to decide whether to step out of bed, put on your bathrobe, reach for your eyeglasses, and bring in the newspaper. Tired yet? Like freeways, routines speed up life's daily transactions by removing the need to stop and decide.

A robust set of routines is a hard-working and efficient component of an organized life. This book helps you identify routines, set them in motion, and bring them to work for you in every area of life.

Organized Spaces

Picture a shoemaker at work—eyes focused on the boot before him, his hands automatically grasp each item he needs as he works. Now send a whirlwind across his workbench, scattering his tools and supplies. Chances are, he'll straighten up and glare at you with an outraged look. You've destroyed his space's ability to support him.

Organized spaces function like that shoemaker's workbench. When focused around our centers of activity, they play a supporting actor's role in the work of our lives. They speed us out the door, keep us focused on the job, or simply allow us to relax.

This book teaches you how to create activity centers, stow your stuff efficiently, and build routines to maintain organized and supportive surroundings.

Well-Managed Time

Each of us enjoys the same amount of time every day, but we vary in how well we live within it. Making appropriate decisions about the use of time and structuring the passing hours so that we achieve what we hope to achieve is the essence of good time management.

People differ in their goals and preferences for the use of time. One person hopes to jump-start work productivity and live life at a faster pace. Another wants to work more efficiently so as to enjoy more hours of leisure spent with family.

Whether you're eager to get more done or to do what you must do more quickly, this book helps you tune your time-management skills. You'll find simple tools and concepts to help you meet your own unique goals for managing time.

Where Do I Begin?

Okay, now that you have some helpful explanations about organization, it's time to jump in and get started. The question is, where to begin?

You can get underway quickly by doing two key things: deciding your initial direction and setting up control central, an activity center to support you as you begin the journey.

Start Where the Shoe Pinches

The road to getting organized begins with a single step, but it's up to you to determine what that first step should be. Because each of us has a different idea of what it means to be organized, and each of us brings varying skills and challenges to the process, your first step needs to be as individual as you are.

Here's a quick way for you to figure out where to begin: start where the shoe pinches—that is, identify a single organizational problem that drives you crazy on a daily basis.

To identify it, sit back in your chair, lace your hands behind your head, and review the events of the last couple days. Are you tired of drinking your morning coffee at a table covered with yesterday's clutter? Have you been hitting the supermarket on the way home from work because there's no food in the refrigerator? Did you sit down to pay the bills, only to realize that they were scattered all over the house, and it took you 20 minutes just to find them?

Wherever the frustration feels highest, that's the place for you to dive in and begin. Choose just one small change to make, such as to declutter a single surface, begin a new routine, or set up a holding container for a certain type of item.

Changing what's bothering you most brings a welcome burst of motivation to carry you forward. Experiencing an immediate reward for fixing your most nagging issue helps keep you going in the direction of a more organized life.

SPEEDY SOLUTION

Mount a hook beside the door you use to enter and exit your home. Make a habit of hanging the keys as soon as you enter the house, and you'll no longer waste a single moment hunting for your key ring. Dog owners get extra credit if they add a second hook for a leash.

Decide on a Target Component

Now that you've made that important first step, you need to choose where to address your first efforts. Focus on the area where you need the most work. Do you need more help controlling clutter, building routines, organizing your space, or managing your time?

When you're mired in a disorganized life, it can be a bit difficult to decide which of the core four represents your biggest challenge. A lot of folks simply throw their hands in the air in response to the question, answering it with a frustrated, "All of them!"

Nevertheless, you'll move the process along more quickly if you focus your efforts on one component at a time and start with your weakest area. Beginning your journey where you need to travel the farthest will have more impact than fine-tuning a skill you've already mastered.

Set Up Control Central

Dealing with the business of your life takes time, energy, and effort. Do you have an appropriate place to help you put it all together? This is control central, your life-management center, the place you'll plan your get-organized journey.

As one part a get-organized activity center and the other part a home office, control central is the place you'll go to handle the business of living. It's where you will work your plan, set goals, and track your progress as you get organized. It will maintain your calendar, checklists, to-do lists, and files. It's where you'll manage your finances, answer correspondence, and access information. Think of it as your base of operations for an organized life.

To set up control central, start by designating an appropriate space. Search your home for a room or area to host command central, but don't get hung up on form. A comfortable chair in a well-lit corner can function just as effectively as a dedicated home office. Some people prefer mobility and can set up control central in a rolling organizer cart so they can work anywhere from sitting at the kitchen table to tucked up in bed. Others may prefer a designated area with a conventional office desk and chair. Figure out what works best for you.

Check the energy level of your designated spot. Do you feel empowered, calm, and comfortable? Is there adequate light for reading, writing, and computer use? A pleasant space makes it easier to carry out the work ahead.

Next, gather the necessary tools and supplies. For an efficient life-management center, you'll want to include the following items:

- Computer and printer
- Flat writing surface
- Calendar or daily planner
- Address book or contacts manager
- Three-ring binders
- Dividers
- Page protectors
- Printer and binder paper
- Pens, pencils, and markers
- File box, file cart, or tabletop file
- Hanging files and/or file folders
- Stamps
- Envelopes and mailing supplies
- Office supplies, such as paper clips, tape, stapler, push pins, and Post-It notes
- Wastebasket

Depending on the space available and personal preference, you can add other items to your control central. A bulletin board or whiteboard can display calendars, shopping lists, reminders, and notes. Music can provide background noise and motivation. Decorative items or houseplants can add ambience.

Your goal is to create a calm, comfortable, supportive place to get on with the business of your organized, productive life. It'll be the launch pad that supports you on your ongoing journey to better home and personal organization.

Gearing Up for Self-Change

Getting organized requires you to make some lasting changes in your life. Whether you want to focus on clutter, time management, or new ways to organize your space, you need to understand the process of self-change in order to succeed.

In this chapter, you explore this process, which includes assessing your organizing preferences, identifying habits that may stand in your way, learning to set and reach goals, and coming to terms with the need for accountability. To get organized fast, understanding how this process works helps you get a grip on what you're asking yourself to do.

Discover Your Organizing Style

Take any two random people, and the way they go about getting organized will differ like night and day. One may be a master of multitasking; the other sticks to one job at a time. One becomes distracted unless surfaces are clear; the other works best with a comfortable level of cozy. To get organized fast, both need to set goals consistent with their innate organizing style.

Your organizing goals will be determined by your unique personality, so let's explore three areas where your personal preferences shape your path to an organized life. Knowing where you fall on each spectrum helps shortcut the process of setting the appropriate goal for you.

Your Clutter Tolerance

Consider this surprising fact: clutter is in the eye of the beholder. There's no single, universal test for a cluttered environment; what looks like a cluttered jumble to one person may be an appealing, cozy setting to another.

Even when you define clutter as items that have no use, no beauty, no value, and no place in your home, the point at which clutter becomes problematic varies from person to person.

For example, a stack of newspapers that wouldn't even register with most people as bothersome will definitely bother a person with a very low clutter tolerance level. In extreme cases, people known as hoarders have a clutter tolerance level so high that they're able to live in a home piled with garbage without feeling the need to deal with their clutter at all.

Clutter tolerance is a spectrum, with some people able to tolerate quite a lot of environmental clutter and others very little. The preference may also operate unconsciously. A low-tolerance person, the one troubled by that stack of newspapers, may not be aware that the cluttered space is the reason he or she is having such a hard time settling in to work.

What's your level of clutter tolerance? It's important to find out, because it represents the sweet spot where you'll aim your organizing efforts. If you tackle more clutter than you need to, you'll be wasting time. If you underestimate your need for clear surfaces, your efforts won't go far enough to fix the problem.

ROAD HAZARD

Keep your eyes firmly on the mirror when you explore your organizing style. Your organized life may not look anything like that lived by friends or family members. Because your personality is unique, your solutions will be, too. Avoid the temptation to measure yourself against others.

Answer these questions to get a clear picture of your level of clutter tolerance:

- If you could have any workspace in the world, what would it look like? Visualize your desk area and your surroundings, and imagine where you'd place your tools and supplies.

- Where are you most effective now? Bring that place to mind, whether it's your kitchen, the computer workspace, or a craft or hobby area. Is it cluttered or clear?

- Think about the homes of your friends. Which one makes you feel most welcome? Is the decorating style closer to cozy country or city chic?

- Where are you when you feel most exasperated in your day-to-day surroundings? What does that place look like?

Your answers to these questions will suggest a level of tolerable clutter that works best for you—the balance of clear space and controlled clutter that makes you feel empowered, effective, and in control. Is your ideal space clear and austere, or does it feature a lively display of tools and décor items? This mental image of your ideal surroundings reflects your clutter tolerance level and signals the right spot to direct your efforts at clutter control.

File It, Pile It, or Deny It?

A second spectrum affects the path you take to get organized: your filing preference. This preference is broader than the word *filing* suggests, since it affects the way you interact with information and materials in many areas of your environment. Even though this preference shows itself everywhere from bathroom cupboards, to office space, to garage storage, the easiest way to get a bead on it is to visualize filing paperwork.

Which one of these three identities feels most comfortable to you?

- The filer
- The piler
- The denier

Filers like their information stored out of view, labeled, and arranged according to some notion of order. Not that filers always have impeccable files—filers actually can falter if they set up overcomplicated systems or fail to create routines for follow-through.

Still, when a filer thinks of getting organized, he or she gravitates to hanging file folders, labeled storage spaces, and closed drawers. Filers work best with their information out of sight yet easily accessible; their systems tend to look like the method most people would consider "organized."

However, here's the paradox: filers are less secure about their ability to retrieve information than the other two filing identities. They feel more comfortable relying on their systems than their memory. A structured information-management system that's easy to use frees a filer to get on with the job.

Pilers, on the other hand, feel uncomfortable when they can't see their stuff. Because a piler wants to keep in visual contact with information, you can spot them by the stacks of files, papers, and books sitting on a desk or placed directly in front of an empty bookcase.

Pilers have a pretty robust idea of where to locate their stuff amid the apparent chaos. If you ask them where to find something, they'll reply, "It's here, somewhere!" They can shuffle a few stacks and pull out what you're looking for.

Pilers perceive order where others see only chaos, as long as they have what they need directly in front of them. Set up a piler with a labeled filing system in a closed drawer, and you're headed for trouble. Even if you train them to use it, they won't. Pilers need the visual cues their stacks provide, and the security of having all their stuff in view. For them, out of sight is truly out of mind.

Working with the piler temperament means finding ways to corral the stacks for easier retrieval and better appearance. Because pilers really do know where things are in their piles and stacks, their filing systems will be less detailed. Where a filer's best friend is a file folder, the piler prefers to associate with a tabletop file or file basket.

 SPEEDY SOLUTION

Hanging file folders make an efficient tool for folks of every filing persuasion. Because it's easier to flip through a horizontal stack than to lift and shift a vertical pile, they offer faster access. Tabbed labels and color coding add immediate visual cues to the location of your stuff.

Deniers find the whole thing just too much work! Like filers, deniers are uncomfortable with messy papers in their workspace, but they're not wild about filing them, either. Result: deniers put off the problem for another day by bundling it all up and sticking it somewhere out of sight. You know a denier by their records boxes and paper sacks of stuff.

Deniers lack both the filer's innate appreciation for organized systems and the piler's internal ability to keep the location of stuff in mind. Overall, deniers simply find tracking their stuff to be much too frustrating.

Deniers respond well to simple information systems and routines that relieve their frustration with their environment. Unlike filers, they won't get bogged down in overly complex systems that take more time to manage than they're worth. And in contrast to pilers, deniers feel relieved when they take steps to keep their stuff both accessible and out of sight.

Coping with the denier preference means taking matters step by step. Deniers need to set up information-management systems, learn to trust them, and craft simple routines to ensure that they use them. Avoiding that frustration meltdown provides a big payoff for the denier preference.

Your Time-Management Style

A third preference that can affect the way you'll get organized is your time-management style. How you perceive the passage of time, how you prefer to tackle a task, and whether you work best under pressure all impact the process of getting organized.

There are no right or wrong answers. What's important is to be aware of your own inclinations. Do you prefer to work toward a tight deadline or to divide a job into measured daily portions? Does multitasking make your day or make your head spin?

Take a look at the following list, and consider where you are in these common measures of time management:

- **Procrastination:** Do you put it off or tackle it early?
- **Scheduling:** Do you slot time by the day, hour, or minute?
- **Pressure:** Do you work best with deadlines or dread them?
- **Focus:** Do you prefer doing one thing at a time or managing a multitude at once?
- **Teamwork:** Do you seek solitude or a supportive team?

- **Pace:** Do you like to take life leisurely or prefer it to be on the go?
- **Rhythm:** Are you a morning person, or do you burn the midnight oil?

Keep your answers in mind as you begin to set goals for your organized life. For example, if you respond well to last-minute pressures, take advantage of that ability by setting intermediate deadlines to spur you on. If you're up with the larks, mind clicking and ready to roll, avoid dribbling away your valuable morning energies with low-priority routines and schedule them for your low-bandwidth afternoons instead. Understanding your time-management style sees to it that you don't waste time on solutions that won't work for you.

Overcoming Personal Roadblocks

When it comes to the process of successful self-change, we can be our own worst enemies. Instead of acting on the desire to get organized, we come up with an array of excuses for why we can't, or we fail to make a goal concrete by devoting time to planning and executing it.

As you start to make changes in your life to get more organized, be on the lookout for these agents of self-sabotage. You'll need to get past them in order to get organized quickly.

 ROAD HAZARD

When you first jump into your new, organized life, put on a pair of blinders. If you stop to survey the entire road ahead of you, it's easy to get discouraged and fall by the wayside. Instead, keep your eyes on what's immediately in front of you, only the next step you need to take. Staying focused on your next action keeps you from being overwhelmed by the entire journey.

Excuses, Excuses

Here you are, determined to find a way to make your life easier and flow more smoothly. You're reading this book, thinking about some changes you'd like to make, and you're getting ready to move forward.

Now enter the excuses. Just at the moment you're poised to take action, excuses operate as a last-ditch effort to prevent change. And oh, how creative they can be! Do these excuses sound familiar?

- I don't have time to get organized.
- Organized people are boring. Who wants to live that way?
- Being organized will stifle my creative side.
- We're going to be moving next year. Why bother?
- I can't afford to buy all those expensive organizing products.

Whether stated in terms of time, money, convenience, or identity, excuses will tap any remotely conceivable rationale to do one simple thing: stop the pending change. Most of us can expect to do battle with them along the way, so be prepared.

To handle excuses, you can safely ignore the particulars of their message. You don't need to debate the excuse or try to counter it. Instead, focus on the messenger and the underlying issue: your fear of change.

When excuses crop up, cut straight to the underlying issue and address it. Tell yourself, "Yes, change is frightening, but I know I can do it!" This cuts the ground right out from under any excuse, no matter how it's stated. Acknowledging the risks and uncertainties that an excuse represents is the best way to send it fading into the background, so you can move past it to better organization.

No Time to Plan? Plan to Fail!

In the telecommunications world, it's called the "last mile problem." For any communications network, the most difficult and expensive segment of the route is always the last mile to the customer's door.

For successful self-change, that difficult last mile is setting aside the time to plan. You can read about getting organized, you can stock up on file folders, you can hang a new calendar on the wall—but until you make time in your day for your organizing program, you're setting yourself up to fail.

Make your organizing desires tangible by devoting time each day to plan and execute your get-organized program. You won't need to give all your time to the job; even segments as small as 15 minutes a day will be enough to bridge that gap between your dream and the reality of a new organized life.

Identifying and Setting Goals

On the road to an organized life, your central task will be to identify, set, and reach a series of goals. To understand the steps involved, look to the game of football. If you play the game the way professionals do, you'll make it to the end zone quickly.

 ROAD HAZARD

When you're excited about making changes in your life, it's easy to take on more than you can manage. Use your energy wisely by working on only one or two goals at a time. By all means, take note of all your goals, and even map out a plan to reach them—just don't try to tackle them all at once. Picking them off one at a time is the fastest way to succeed.

Define the Goal

On a football field, the goal is always clearly defined: goalposts mark the target of the team's efforts. On the road to better organization, you'll travel fastest if you define clear, specific goals along the way.

Replace vague, undefined aims such as "I want to be a better financial manager" with statements that make your goal clear and specific, such as, "I will pay bills twice a month and review my finances every quarter." Knowing exactly what the goal requires is the first step to reaching it.

Break It Down

A football team is always aware of where they stand in relation to the goal because each section of the field is clearly marked. Put this principle to work for you by dividing your goals into daily, weekly, and long-term steps to track your progress. Marking the path to completion by breaking it down into small chunks makes quick work of a larger, more complicated goal.

Face the Goal

A football team plays the game facing the goal; all their actions are directed to the end zone. You need to do the same thing. Face your goal of better organization by moving it out of the realm of talk and speculation, and get it working in your daily life.

For instance, when our friend the financial manager starts paying bills on a regular daily and weekly basis, he's on the road to achieving his goal.

Study Setbacks

A football team always analyzes its performance after the game so that coaches and players can learn from their mistakes.

When your goals fail or fade on you, take the time to figure out why. This is an important exercise because what you learn teaches you what not to do next time. Accept that setbacks happen, then learn from them and begin again, better prepared to reach the goal.

SPEEDY SOLUTION

To keep your goals in front of you, write the three or four most important ones on an index card. Keep it with you every day in your purse or wallet, and each time you see the card, it'll remind you to stay the course. Multiply the motivation by taping a copy to your bathroom mirror, refrigerator, and computer.

Self-Coaching and Accountability

As with any other kind of self-change, getting organized can be a lonely business. Everyone works better with a little pat on the back from time to time. Feedback and support, whether from ourselves or from others, is an integral part of successful self-change. Make coaching and accountability part of your get-organized program, and it will strengthen and speed the process.

Be Your Own Cheerleader

With self-coaching, you become your own partner on the path to getting organized. By consciously donning a second hat—that of coach—you expand your view beyond the immediate object of the process, such as organizing the kitchen shelves, to include an awareness of how well you are working the process. Adding that level of accountability strengthens the process and makes you more likely to succeed.

Self-coaching is convenient, free, and empowering. As coach, you identify your objectives, create an action plan, and review your actions after you carry them out. Just as a coach would reward a player, you can reward yourself, too, and celebrate forward progress with small incentives. You'll focus on accountability and feedback, not just on the stacks and piles. It's a broader, more effective way to reach the organizing goals in your life.

Finding Support from Others

Feedback and support from others can be valuable as you get organized. Supportive friends can understand what you're going through, help you sort out issues, and cheer you on when you succeed.

Online support groups, 12-step groups such as Clutterers Anonymous, or social networking connections can boost your efforts to get organized. Check out Appendix A for a listing of support groups for getting organized.

Don't overlook the help offered by consultants and therapists. Professional organizers can teach you to clear your clutter, help you set up systems, and establish routines in record time. A therapist's help can be especially useful when organizing issues coexist with conditions like attention deficit disorders (ADD/ADHD) or obsessive-compulsive disorder (OCD). These options, while not free, may be a solution to help speed you on your way.

Kicking Clutter to the Curb

Clutter. We know it when we see it, and we see it everywhere! Plastic shopping bags swell like bread dough underneath the kitchen sink. Stacks of mail reproduce with abandon on counters and tabletops. Food-storage containers avalanche at us when the cabinet door is opened. Composed of once-useful items whose time has come and gone, clutter washes up around us in every area of life.

It's safe to say that most of us will have "clear clutter" on our list of get-organized goals. The question is, what's the fastest way to cut clutter once and for all?

In this chapter, we explore the root cause of clutter, learn a short and simple method to tackle it, and plan a whole-house assault to clear it out of our surroundings.

Causes of Clutter

No matter what its outward form, every item of clutter is produced by a single cause: a deferred decision. Simply put, clutter is the result of our failure to decide. Whether we delay a decision, deny the need to make it, or defer taking action on that decision, the genesis of clutter lies in the deciding.

Take a look around you to see the proof of this. Junk mail sprawls on the countertop a few short feet from the recycling bin because the person who brought in the mail failed to sort and dispose of it. Too-small clothing crowds the clothes closet, waiting for its owner to admit that it no longer fits. Empty cans of paint hang out in the garage, in need of a lift to the disposal center.

While you'll find a deferred decision behind clutter of all kinds, the principle of it plays itself out in three variations: delayed decision making, deferred action, and denial. Let's take a look at these factors and see if you can recognize them at work in your own surroundings.

Delayed Decision Making

Around the house, it's hard to find a better example of delayed decision making than old school textbooks. Once you pack away the cap and gown, they have no more use in your life, yet here they are, taking up space on the bookshelf or piled in a corner.

You can't release them because you can't decide what to do with them. They were expensive, so should you sell them? How about donating them to the local library? Maybe you should keep them, because someday you might need to look something up. Making a decision seems too difficult, so the textbooks stay put, taking up space, gathering dust, and growing steadily more out-of-date with each passing year.

Blast through delayed decision making by asking yourself this question: what's the worst that can happen if I release this item? Most of the time, that worst-case scenario means little more than having to buy another book (or look the issue up online). So release the clutter, reclaim your space, and move on!

Deferring Action

Some clutter is born not from lack of a decision, but because we fail to follow through with the decisions we make. For example, few of us will read or reread newspapers that are more than a couple days old. When we put them down, we've already decided to dispose of them. Nonetheless, they wander the house, silent witnesses to our failure to take follow-up action by walking them to the recycling bin.

Disposal routines can go a long way toward addressing the problem of deferred action. Adding a collection container to the family room and creating a routine of emptying it once a week makes quick work of scattered newspapers. The hard part is deciding to release the clutter, so disposal routines are helpful in automating the end of the road and sending the clutter on its merry way.

SPEEDY SOLUTION

When you can't see the clutter for the trees, borrow a pair of sharper eyes and tackle clutter with a trusted friend. Outsiders to your space see clutter more clearly, to help you release it from your life.

Denial

When it comes to clutter, denial is like putting on a pair of rose-colored glasses. Clutter? What clutter? That's my stuff! Denial blocks the realization that you need to make a decision in the first place.

Yes, the closet is stuffed with leftover materials from a long-ago fling with scrapbooking, but you're not yet ready to admit that you've grown tired of stamps and stickers and glitter. Denial keeps us from seeing that items we no longer need, use, or value have swallowed our space and surroundings.

Denial is the most difficult-to-address variant of the causes of clutter. It's easy to spot with hoarders, but most of the rest of us possess a good bit of it as well. Because denial keeps us from recognizing clutter as an issue to be dealt with, it postpones the day of reckoning. To counter denial, we need to have our clutter vision checked … and corrected.

To stare down denial, ask yourself, "Is this item part of my life now?" Maintaining a museum of the outgrown, whether it's clothing, hobbies, or stage of life, makes it harder to live the life you have now. Remind yourself that your spaces should support you in the life you live now, and release those holdovers from another day.

The STOP Clutter Method

The STOP clutter method is an easy way to help you make otherwise difficult decisions about your clutter. Working with short bites of time, STOP clutter sessions force decision making, bring order to a space, and ensure that the survivors are all organized and put away before the session is over.

The name helps you remember the steps to this clutter-clearing method. To STOP clutter, follow this sequence:

1. **S**ort items into needed and unneeded categories.

2. **T**oss unneeded items into collection boxes.

3. **O**rganize the survivors.

4. **P**ut away out-of-place items.

These four steps keep you grounded as you work through each STOP clutter session. Because each session is short (between 15 and 30 minutes long), fatigue won't drag down your ability to make good decisions. Each STOP clutter session limits decluttering to a small, specific space, so you won't tear apart more area than you can organize and return to functional quickly. Bite by bite, STOP clutter sessions make it easy to conquer clutter around the house.

To STOP clutter, start by assembling a toolkit. You'll need four boxes or open containers into which you'll sort your stuff. They should be large, lightweight, and easy to handle—records boxes from the office supply store make ideal STOP clutter containers.

Label your boxes as follows:

- Put Away—for things that belong somewhere else
- Give Away—for items to be donated to charity
- Store—for items that need to be placed in storage
- Throw Away—for recycling or trash

The labels lay out decision-making options for each item you'll handle as you tackle cluttered spaces. The decision-blasting rule is that, once you pick up an item, you can put it down only inside one of the boxes, forcing a decision.

 ROAD HAZARD

> While it's possible to dispose of unwanted items by selling them online or holding a garage sale, this decision option adds an unnecessary layer of complexity to the decluttering process. To cut clutter quickly, the fewer options you give yourself, the better. Deliver the surplus to a charity collection point, and skip the yard sale, to keep things simple … and fast.

Next, add a timer. While you can use your phone or the timer on your microwave to time your STOP clutter sessions, a standard kitchen timer with a nice loud tick offers the most motivation. The sound will be a subliminal reminder to speed your decluttering session.

Now with your toolkit at the ready, it's time to begin. Gather your four boxes and your timer, and select an area to have a STOP clutter session. Set your timer for 20 minutes, and begin.

Consider an example: the cabinet beneath the kitchen sink. Place your boxes around your workspace, open the cabinet door, and remove every item from the cabinet. You'll *sort* as you work, setting the cleansers, sprayers, and sponges that belong in the space to one side.

To deal with the remaining items, *toss* them into one of the four boxes. Here's a pair of pliers, last used in an emergency faucet repair. They belong not beneath the sink, but in the toolbox, so tuck them into the "Put Away" box. A wad of plastic shopping bags goes straight to the "Throw Away" box. The recycling containers that were too inconvenient to use are entrusted to the "Give Away" box, and the kitchen-counter Christmas decoration hiding in the back corner takes a short trip to the "Store" box.

When the cabinet is empty, it's time to *organize*. Clean the empty cabinet first by wiping it out; then make a quick assessment of how to best organize the items that belong in there. Place the most-used items nearest the door, and send the seasonal cleaners, like silver polish, to the back of the space.

When the timer rings, it's time to stop what you're doing to *put away* the results of your work. Grab the "Put Away" box and circle the house, returning items to their appropriate places. Dump the "Give Away" box into a garbage bag, and set it aside for donation.

Items to be stored should be taken as close to their eventual home as possible and placed in a catchall "To Be Stored" container near the entrance to the attic or storage area. Finally, empty the "Throw Away" box into the garbage can.

Store your STOP clutter boxes and dust off your hands with pride. You did it!

SPEEDY SOLUTION

Make quick work of floating clutter with a clutter sweep! When you have a couple minutes, grab a garbage bag and sweep through the house, grabbing empty water bottles, junk mail, and crumpled receipts as quickly as you can. When two minutes are up or the bag is full, dump it in the trash, dust your hands, and kiss that clutter good-bye.

The Clear-a-Thon

Working one small bite at a time, the STOP clutter method keeps you on track as you cut clutter in closets, cupboards, and drawers. But what do you do when you need to conquer disorder across the entire house? Enter the clutter clear-a-thon: a coordinated plan of attack to bring clutter under control in a larger area.

The clear-a-thon bridges the gap between small clutter-clearing sessions and the larger goal of a clutter-free home. While the actual work will be done with a series of STOP clutter sessions, the clear-a-thon coordinates storage options and provides space to shuffle your stuff, to speed up the job.

Assessing Household Storage Options

You can declutter your heart out with STOP clutter sessions, but when you're dealing with an entire home, you need to stand back a bit to get the big picture. Assessing your storage options and crafting a whole-house plan to stow your stuff is the route to a well-organized home.

With paper and a pen, or a phone with dictation capability, size up the options for storage in your surroundings. Start at the front door and walk around your home, noting each closet, cupboard, or chest of drawers that offers storage potential. Peek inside and take note of what your storage spaces currently contain.

Chances are, you're going to find a mix of effective storage and dysfunctional space. Make note of what's working and what's not. For example, the coat closet is crammed with sporting goods, the spare leaf from the dining room table, and some sacks of assorted junk mail. A STOP clutter session will bring usability back to the closet, but you'll need to find storage space for the items you're going to remove from the closet.

Be on the lookout for empty space. An unused shelf at the top of your child's closet can hold winter blankets or boxes of out-of-season clothing. Black-hole areas in kitchen cabinets offer storage opportunities for holiday dishes you use only once a year. Note these empty spaces so that you remember them and can use them when needed.

Circle the house to assess all your storage space options. The goal is to get an idea of what stuff you have to be stored and what options you have to store it. Craft a quick what-goes-where plan to guide your clear-a-thon.

Setting Up Temporary Holding Areas

Your whole-house assessment will likely show that some of your storage areas are not working to capacity. An easy-to-access closet would work well as a linen closet, but right now, it's a repository for boxes of seasonal décor. Those boxes belong in the attic ... but not until after you've made space for them by sorting out all the children's outgrown clothes currently taking up that space in the attic.

ROAD HAZARD

Don't let the temporary storage places become a permanent home for items in transit! Finish the job, or you'll face having to start all over again a few weeks or months down the road.

When you're ready to shift items around, set up temporary holding areas designed for short-term housing of storage in transit. A section of empty wall space, a clear spot in the garage, or an unused guest room can become temporary storage central—the place where you'll house the strays and orphans on the road to their eventual storage home.

To make the transition process run smoothly, sort storage-in-transit items by category and label them. For example, label boxes holding bedding and linens and those holding potential hand-me-downs so they don't get intertwined. Then as you declutter and clear each permanent storage area, you'll know where to find the contents that belong there.

SPEEDY SOLUTION

Mount an over-the-door shoe bag on the back of a door to sort and organize seasonal items. Gloves and hats in the winter, or sandals and sunscreen in the summer fit handily into shoe-size pockets and help speed the family out the door.

Sustaining the Clutter Clear-a-Thon

Now that you've got a pretty good idea of what stuff you have to be stored and where you want to store it, the trick is to stay the course. To make sure your noble effort doesn't burn too bright and flare out on you, try these ideas to sustain your clutter clear-a-thon:

1. **Dive in daily.** Even a 5- or 10-minute mini-session can free your desk from pens that don't write and curling layers of faded Post-It notes. Progress begets progress, so keep your get-organized goal moving forward by tackling a STOP clutter session every day.

2. **Aim your efforts.** Cutting clutter and shifting storage often goes faster if you stick to one category at a time. Tackling your own clothes closet means you'll bring stronger energy to sorting out garments in the children's room. Also, working by category makes it easier to craft successful storage solutions. For example, with all out-of-season clothing stored together in the same location, you'll spend less time changing out seasonal clothing when the time comes.

3. **Cultivate your support system.** Share your successes with a trusted friend or with members of a declutter support group. They will understand the satisfaction you feel when you finally get to the bottom of a mess. Accept their cheers graciously; their support will bring you a burst of energy to keep the process moving forward.

4. **Review your progress.** When the pace of change slows, it can be motivating to look back and see how far you've come. If you find your energies flagging, tour your newly decluttered spaces. Reviewing your progress can rekindle the desire to spread the changes to every corner of the house and can hoist you over the hump.

 ROAD HAZARD

Burnout is an occupational hazard for those who want to banish clutter. When we finally gear up to conquer it, we often go too far, emptying an entire closet in a single afternoon. The result is, we're navigating piles of old prom dresses for weeks to come. Cut clutter in short, sustainable sessions, to be sure you're able to finish what you start.

Establishing Clutter Preserves

As you take whole-house aim on clutter, keep one thing in mind: there's no such thing as clutter-free living. Sweeping up scattered remote controls, game disks, and toys from the family coffee table one day won't prevent the household from reestablishing a nearly identical clutter constellation a day or so later.

As we live, we kick up a certain amount of clutter in our wake. It's an inevitable by-product of daily life. Accept this reality by setting up clutter preserves—specific areas where clutter is permitted, contained, and controlled. By creating designated places for clutter to settle on the fly, you keep it from floating freely and depositing itself at random around the house.

Clutter preserves express the principle of contained clutter. In the family room, a few low, flat baskets go a long way toward containing clutter in the form of remotes, video game controllers, reading materials, and children's playthings. At the end of each video game session of saving the world, the gamers can just toss controllers into the basket, where they're accessible yet contained.

Also, don't turn your nose up at the idea of a junk drawer. True, you'll want to have only one, but it's the place to sweep things like rubber bands, shopping receipts, clipped coupons, and unidentified keys. Clearing it out regularly with a scheduled STOP clutter session keeps the junk drawer functioning as a versatile and useful clutter preserve.

Here are some suggestions for setting up clutter preserves:

- A basket by the back door can hold mittens and scarves in winter, flip-flops and sun hats in summer.
- Tossed clothing is okay in bedrooms, as long as it confines itself to the bedroom chair.
- A shoebox-size plastic storage container can be home to hardware bits and pieces in the garage.

- Children's toys find a good home in living areas when they're confined to color-coded plastic baskets, one per child.

- A small box on a closet shelf keeps safety pins, spare buttons, and collar tabs close at hand.

Just as with wildlife, clutter is welcome to roam freely inside the preserve's boundaries, but if it sets one toe outside, it's fair game for disposal. Keep that division operational, and the clutter confined, for the principle to work.

Clutter Doesn't Live Here Anymore

The fight against clutter is more like a war than a battle. No matter how well and decisively you evict it, clutter will keep coming back, trying to put a foot in the door and take up residence again.

How do you keep clutter from coming back? By addressing the inner voices that slow clutter decision making, creating checkpoints to release clutter as you go, and adopting new ways to live in which less is more.

Conquering Your Clutter Demons

Clutter is a product of deferred decision making; it piles up around us because we can't or won't decide to release it when its time has come. If all we need to do is jump in and decide, why is it so hard? It's because of clutter demons—internal voices that make us hesitate in our dealings with our stuff.

Lodged deep in our personalities, these inner voices prevent us from making swift and smart clutter decisions. They tap into fears and insecurities that prevent change, even when those changes are in our own best interest.

The solution? Know your enemy! Addressing the hidden voices behind the failure to decide can create a powerful surge in your ability to deal with clutter. Let's explore the clutter demons that speak to you … and how you can silence them.

Sentiment

Sentiment suffers from a fatal confusion that a physical thing stands in the same place as the memories associated with it. Hence the panicked fluttering many of us feel when it's time to release mementos such as ticket stubs, greeting cards, or children's artwork.

To tone down the voice of this clutter demon, remind yourself that the stuff is a symbol, not the reality. A birthday card is not the friend who sent it; the concert program is not the wonderful evening you had at the performance.

You can choose to cherish a memory without finding room for every single item associated with it. When you're decluttering sentimental items, select the best and brightest reminder, and release the remaining items so they don't dilute the meaning by becoming clutter.

SPEEDY SOLUTION

Instead of preserving each sentimental item associated with a memory, photograph it. Better yet, have a friend or family member snap the item as you hold it, use it, or wear it. Save the photo in an album or scrapbook, adding a short note describing what it means to you. This way you save the memories, not the clutter.

Scarcity Thinking

Scarcity thinking is rooted in the fear that resources may not be available in the future. Grounded in insecurity, this clutter demon rushes to the defense of empty yogurt containers and stacks of unread magazines, shouting, "But I might need those someday!"

Reach for a realistic view of resources to counter this inner voice. If you need yogurt containers, you can find them in gleaming rows at the supermarket. Old magazines? They're living the good life at the local library. Reminding yourself that resources are readily available can go a long way to silence scarcity thinking.

Perfectionism

Perfectionism prevents change by erecting impossible standards. Crafty enough to put it in terms like "a job worth doing is worth doing well," this inner voice insists that no action be taken unless and until it can be done to perfection.

A bulging dresser drawer in need of a good decluttering is a good example. Perfectionism dictates that not a single worn-out sock be touched until you buy scented drawer liners and make time to organize all four drawers in the dresser perfectly.

The problem is, this isn't a perfect world. It's better to reach for an imperfect solution than to offer no solution at all. To fight the voice of perfectionism, remind yourself that "good enough" is a good enough goal for anyone. Who needs "perfect," anyway?

Procrastination

Procrastination knows that change won't occur if you never make it to the starting line. To prevent that all-important first step, this inner voice reels off excuse after excuse to persuade you to put off dealing with your clutter.

You're too busy. You're too tired. Things will go faster tomorrow … or the day after that … or next year. Procrastination offers any excuse necessary to keep you from making a beginning.

The solution is to plug your ears and make a start. Jumping into action hurdles right over procrastination's fear of change, and the momentum of getting started often provides enough energy to carry you all the way to the finish line.

Rebellion

Rebellion is an inner voice that chafes against powerlessness. Often arising from childhood conflicts, this clutter demon may also channel voices of blame and resentment to prevent you from disposing of clutter.

Rebellion sulks, pouts, and mutters, "I don't want to, and you can't make me!" or "It's not my mess, why should I?" whenever a clutter decision is on the table.

The solution here is to realize that it's time to grow up! The quickest way to shortcut this clutter demon is to trade places with the authority figure in the shadows. Remind rebellion that it's no longer Mom or anyone else who wants a clean and organized house: it's you.

The Miser

The miser believes that any prior investment in an item must be protected at all costs, even when conditions have changed and that value has dissipated. This clutter demon will splutter, "But I paid $2,000 for that!" when faced with the need to release a broken computer built in the last century.

To silence this inner voice, broaden your sense of value. Purchase price is only one indicator of what an item is really worth; others include current market value and the ongoing cost required to house the unit. Stay nimble and flexible about the notion of value to shortcut the miser's objections.

SPEEDY SOLUTION

Modern technology provides a quick reality check when struggling with issues of value. Is your book a penny title or a collectible edition? Find out fast at Amazon. What will people really pay for that college-era set of bookcase speakers? You'll know in a minute if you look them up on eBay. Smartphone apps can scan bar codes to give a quick read on the actual value of surplus stuff.

Setting Up Clutter Checkpoints

Clutter control would be a walk in the park if we could spot clutter for what it is at the outset of our association and kick it to the curb then and there. The problem is that clutter is made, not born, and the timeline for the transformation varies. A favorite magazine could slide into the clutter category in a year or two, while children's clothing and toys will make the transition even sooner.

As tempting as the idea is, you can't prevent future clutter by barring the door against any and all potential candidates. Instead, establish clutter checkpoints—a set of habits and practices designed to ease newly crowned clutter out of your life on a regular basis.

Clutter checkpoints have two things going for them. First, they represent an educated guess on the point at which an item moves from "useful" to "clutter." For example, deciding that you'll release an item if you haven't used it in a year makes a pretty good stab at setting that point; if you just follow the rule, you're spared a lot of decisional back-and-forth.

Second, checkpoints make clutter release automatic. You don't have to think about it, decide about it, or get worked up about it. The checkpoint operates to dispose of the newly minted offenders with a minimum of drama.

To create a checkpoint, you rely on space, time, or conditions to set limits for an item's tenure in your home. When the space is filled, the time is up, or the conditions are met, it's time to toss.

 ROAD HAZARD

While most clutter consists of once-useful items whose time has come and gone, there are notable exceptions. Even when new novelties and mass-produced souvenirs teeter right on the edge of the clutter abyss, these items have precious little value from the get-go. If you let them into your life, be prepared for their immediate descent into clutter. Spare yourself and have your giggle at the "singing fish wall plaque" while at the store … and leave it there.

Designate Space

Space is the simplest way to define a clutter checkpoint. For items that pile up quickly, such as newspapers, designate a container or a space to hold the pending clutter candidates. When the container is full, it's emptied, or the oldest contents are removed to make space for new issues.

Here are some space-based examples for creating clutter checkpoints:

- Assign magazines a home in a basket or magazine holder from the office supply store. When the holder is full, remove and toss the oldest issue each time a new one arrives.

- In entertainment areas, set shelf space limits for books, CDs, and DVDs. Once shelving fills up, any new addition to the collection must take the place of an older title released for donation.

- In the kitchen, control the number of giveaway items like coffee mugs or commemorative glasses by limiting the cupboard space assigned to them. With every foot race, the family runner will need to part with an old water bottle to make space for a new one.

- A makeup organizer can help rein in cosmetic clutter in the bathroom. Choose an organizer with separate compartments for lipstick, compacts, and pencils; after a trip to the cosmetics counter, older items will have to yield space to the newcomers.

- Prevent a population explosion of stuffed animals in children's rooms with a "stuffie hammock." Buy and mount a small mesh hammock in the corner above a child's bed. All the fuzzy friends that can crowd into the hammock (and stay there!) are welcome to hang around—the rest need to hit the road in search of a new place to call home.

Set the Time

Time harnesses the power of calendaring to automate clutter checkpoints. When you link clutter-cutting sessions to events around the year, it's easier to keep clutter under control.

Try these time-based checkpoints to schedule clutter removal on a regular basis:

- Add "Clear 20" to your list of New Year's resolutions. Moving throughout the house, create 20 percent of free space in closets, cupboards, drawers, and shelves. By clearing out an arbitrary 20 percent of existing items at the beginning of each year, you'll make room for holiday gifts and the new possessions that will come your way in the months ahead.

- At summer's end, evaluate sporting goods, picnic supplies, and gardening items before storing them for winter. Whether it's a lawn chair with rump-sprung webbing, an air mattress that won't hold air, or a cracked and peeling planter, cull the clutter candidates now.

- Add a preholiday "toy clear-out" to each year's holiday celebration. Together with your children, assess the state of their current toys. Remove broken or inoperative playthings, and help them choose a few items in good condition to give to toy drives. You'll get a good feel for gift suggestions, encourage your child to give, and see to it that the season's new toys will have a place to go after the gift boxes are unwrapped.

SPEEDY SOLUTION

With clutter, as with people, breaking up is hard to do, and it's even harder early in a relationship. Look for natural endings to establish clutter checkpoints. For example, it's easier to toss broken lights and tattered ornaments when putting away the tree after the holidays, or to pitch stained T-shirts when you're packing the summer clothes away in the fall. Use the momentum at the end of the road to cut seasonal clutter.

Set Conditions

Conditions can be great fun; they're nifty little agreements you make with yourself to usher clutter out the door whenever a certain condition arises. Often tied to acquiring new stuff, condition-based checkpoints can be very effective in the war against clutter. Because the newcomer in the house distracts your attention, there's less resistance to clearing out the old.

People who stay clutter free often rely on condition-based checkpoints like the following to stay on track:

- "One in, one out" puts a natural limit on clutter of all kinds. Buy a new white shirt? One old one must be removed from the closet. Find a great sale on bed sheets? Pull an older set out of your linen closet to compensate. The goal is to create equilibrium between incoming and outgoing items. To step up the pace of clutter removal, try "one in, two out"!

- A hanger checkpoint sorts out a clothes closet effortlessly over the course of a single season. To establish it, when changing out seasonal clothing, simply reverse every hanger's direction on the clothing rod so that the hanger's hook points back-to-front. As you wear and return your clothes to the closet, hang them as you would ordinarily. At season's end, anything left draped on a reversed hanger goes straight to donation, not to storage; it's been identified as clutter, not as clothing.

- In this day of online shopping, a "shipping box challenge" offers a clever mechanism to keep clutter at bay. Instead of flattening shipping boxes for recycling, when they arrive, fill them with donations and deliver them to a local charity. This checkpoint is particularly useful during the holiday season—and ensures that the household won't see a clutter surge after the gifts have been opened.

- Want to get natural human competitiveness on your side to help clear clutter? Try a clutter pact with another household member, challenging them to meet or beat your clutter tally. You release a box of old college textbooks, they release a stack of '80s record albums, and both of you enjoy the extra space and more serene atmosphere of the home you share together.

- "Use it or lose it" can be a useful checkpoint to sort out specialty craft equipment, tools, or cookware. For these seldom-used items, set a reasonable time period—say, one year—and promise yourself that you will release items you haven't used in that time. If you haven't baked a cake in the shape of a teddy bear in a year, you never will, so find the pan a new home with nice people who will love it.

ROAD HAZARD

A donation box or bag is a powerful tool for releasing clutter … if you can keep yourself from having second thoughts about the items it contains. Resist the temptation to undo your decisions by keeping donations out of sight and out of mind. Seal boxes with package tape as you fill them. Use black plastic garbage bags, not clear ones, and tie them too tightly to be reopened once they're full.

Exploring Deacquisition Strategies

Making faster decisions and setting up clutter checkpoints helps you cope with clutter on an ongoing basis, but to decrease the flow at the source, you'll need to address the desire to acquire.

Finding ways to live well with less stuff not only clears out the cluttered landscape, but also enhances the life you live. Fewer possessions means fewer decisions to make, more space to enjoy, and more time and money to spend on the things that matter most. Try these deacquisition strategies to put this principle into play.

Borrow, Don't Buy

Planning a new project, many of us automatically reach for the shopping list to stock up on tools and supplies. As a result, our closets are full of items like bow makers, tile cutters, and cake stands—specialized equipment we've used once or twice and never touched again. As a clutter-cutting rule of thumb, borrow, don't buy, any item that you will use fewer than 10 times.

Lending options for single-use or specialized tools are all around us. Interested in a new hobby? Check out the local photography club, bird-watching group, or woodworking club; many organizations offer loaner equipment for use by beginners. Similarly, adult education classes provide access to sewing machines, cake-decorating supplies, and tools for furniture repair.

Don't overlook commercial solutions. Planning a party? Party rental firms offer everything you'd need, from tablecloths to glassware. Home improvement retailers often lend tools necessary for a project when you purchase supplies; at the crafts store, you can often use specialty tools if you buy materials there.

Utilize Online Access

Taking advantage of the digital age is a great solution to the conundrum of collecting "too much stuff." Whether it's music or movies, books or crafts patterns, it's no longer necessary to house your own physical collection of these items in order to have access to them.

You can access a massive movie collection by using DVD services like Netflix or by tapping online streaming from your cable provider. Instead of buying physical CDs, move to digital copies, tune in to internet radio stations, or join "all you can listen" music subscription services. E-book readers make it easy to tote a large library wherever you go and prevent last season's bestsellers from piling up around the house.

Even patterns for knitting, sewing, and crafts are now available through online libraries. Whether it's plastic canvas or quilting, you can find a bonanza of ideas and instruction without having to touch a shelf of books.

Make the Most of What You Have

What's a good way to shortcut the desire for the latest-and-greatest electronic gadget or new must-have kitchen appliance? Read the manual for the version you currently have!

Most of us fail to use our devices to their full potential. Have you mastered more than the basic functions of your smartphone, DVD player, or food processor?

Before rushing out to answer the call of a new device, check out the possibilities of the one you currently own. Often, using what you have more fully can satisfy your need for change.

Buy Good Once

When rearing young children, home-baked cookies were a staple of our household. During that time, we burned out mixers at the rate of about one a year. Buying not-quite-adequate equipment left us with a cupboard full of parts and accessories known as the mixer graveyard.

Only when we bit the bullet and invested in a powerful and pricey stand mixer was the problem resolved. That mixer still sits on our kitchen counter today, a testament to the value of buying good once.

Put this principle to work around your house. In the closet, a well-made jacket constructed from quality materials will give good service years after its trendy, cheap cousin has departed for the ragbag. In the garage, one set of craftsman-quality tools will outlive and outperform a steady succession of bargain-bin tool kits. In the kitchen, a single set of fine knives can be sharpened regularly for a lifetime of use.

Buy good once, and you'll save yourself a lot of clutter decisions along the way.

Habits, Routines, and Activity Centers

Chapter

5

In This Chapter

- Putting habits to work for you
- Tapping the power of routines to speed daily life
- Creating activity centers to focus spaces

Sit back and bring to mind the most organized person you know. Each of us has one: a friend or neighbor who seems to be free of the chaos and clutter that have us limping along. Whether with home, office, or family life, these lucky souls seem to have it all together, all the time.

What's their secret? It's household help, in the form of habits, routines, and activity centers. Chances are, your organized friend relies on a robust set of automated behaviors and organized spaces to support his or her daily activities.

To join them, you'll want to create new habits, develop timesaving routines, and establish household activity centers to make life flow more smoothly. Working together, these three organizing concepts speed and streamline day-to-day living.

Getting Your Habits on Your Side

When it comes to getting things done, a habit is the shortest distance between two points. Habits operate like a tractor beam, propelling us forward without thought or volition. Because they short-circuit the need to stop and decide, habits are a powerful tool for an organized life.

Don't believe habits are powerful? Just try to break a bad one! Once established, habits sail along forever, getting the job done quickly and without further thought. Most of the time, you're barely aware of their presence as they lead you through the dance of life.

To get organized fast, you'll want to build a stable of helpful habits to speed up day-to-day activities. Putting the power of habits to work for you is an essential element of an organized life.

Anatomy of a Habit

What makes a habit so powerful? Recent scientific research has zeroed in on what happens when a habit is in play. Understanding the process can help us create good habits and extinguish the bad ones that hold us back.

A habit begins with a trigger, a cue that signals the start of a chain of behaviors. For example, the thud of the newspaper hitting the front porch can trigger a morning ritual: getting up, drinking coffee, and reading the paper. The sound is the cue that sets the habit in motion.

Next comes the habit's routine: the set of activities that constitutes the work of the habit. For our newspaper reader, that routine consists of arising from bed, retrieving the paper, adding coffee and water to the coffee pot, and pushing the brew button. He or she doesn't need to think about finding the coffee filters or counting the number of scoops because habit has taken over. The behaviors proceed automatically, on autopilot, without conscious decision.

Finally, the habit delivers a reward. The first sip of aromatic coffee, enjoyed while scanning the headlines, reinforces the willingness to set the habit in motion. Scientists tell us that a spike in brain activity accompanies this reward, which accounts for the persistence of habit. Once a habit is in place, we'll do almost anything to get that reward, and each time we repeat the cycle, we strengthen the habit's place in our life.

ROAD HAZARD

Old habits don't die—they just bide their time. If you're replacing a habit, the new habit will need to offer a substitute for the reward you've been getting from the old one. It's not enough to decide that a bad habit has to go; you'll need to push it aside by adopting a healthier alternative that meets the same need.

Understanding the cycle of trigger, routine, and reward gives us the tools we need to create new and stronger habits as quickly as possible.

To get a new habit off to a good start, focus on the benefit you expect to receive. Many times, the habit itself generates a reward, like that first sip of coffee, but if a reward doesn't seem obvious, create one.

For example, if you plan to clear the kitchen counters daily, imagine the pleasure you'll have each evening as you stand back and admire your clean and organized space. If you've decided to pay bills weekly, schedule the session so you can conclude it just before a favorite television program. Turning on the set and relaxing on the couch will be your reward. Focus on a payoff to strengthen each new habit you'll put into play.

Next, consider the trigger, the cue you'll use to signal the start of the new habit. Some habits are triggered by outside events, such as the arrival of the paper on the porch. Other habits need to begin with a specific opening action to signal your brain, "Hey! Stand back, a habit's on the way!"

Finally, give some thought to the meat of your habit—the routine. This is the get-it-done phase of the habit, bundling a series of steps and actions into one automatic flow. The routine carried out by a habit can be short and sweet or lengthy and complex. Set your habit in motion by being specific about the steps you want your habit's routine to include.

To put new habits to work for you quickly, keep these tips in mind:

- Set a concrete, specific goal.
- Identify the habit's trigger.
- List each step the habit should carry out.
- Start small and add more steps later.
- Associate a reward to reinforce the habit.
- Practice the habit daily.
- Expect it to take a month to cement the habit.

To establish new habits quickly, take them on one at a time. Because the effort is all in the front end, be sure each new habit is firmly established before you move on to the next one.

SPEEDY SOLUTION

Habits are a lot like trains: one engine can pull many cars. Adding steps to a habit you already have takes less time and effort than cranking up a whole new habit. To get organized fast, expand existing habits by adding new actions to their routines.

Habits for an Organized Life

Ask organized people how they stay on top of things, and they're apt to give you a puzzled look and say something like, "I don't know, I just do it!" Even though they rely on a full roster of good habits, the stealthy nature of habit formation can cause them to draw a blank when asked about the specifics of their orderly lives.

Watch organized people in action, and you'll see their story: good habits are evidenced everywhere. Leaving a room, they straighten the newspapers and gather scattered belongings on their way out the door. When cooking, they wipe up spills and tidy counters on the fly. Before bed, they lay out clothing to wear the next day, work materials, and makings for lunch. Without thinking about it, their habits kick in to keep disorganization at bay on an hourly basis.

Do you want to join their ranks? Then work to incorporate these habits into your everyday life:

- Make a place for everything, and put everything in its place.
- Clean up as you go along.
- Sort the mail over the trashcan.
- Tidy each room as you leave it.
- When you use something, put it back.
- Toss trash immediately.
- Clean up after each task before you begin a new one.
- Each night, make a plan for the following day.

Building Routines into Daily Life

Behind each organized life, you'll find a posse of routines at work to keep things running smoothly. Yes, I know—routines sound about as exciting as housedresses and sensible shoes, but their mundane nature belies their power. Trust me, you'll come to love them, homely or not.

A morning routine speeds parents of small children out the door (without forgetting the diapers, pacifier, or naptime blanket). A pretravel routine shuts off the hot water, stops mail and news-paper delivery, and alerts the neighbors to your absence so that you leave for vacation with an easy mind. Cleaning routines for each day, week, and season ensure that the house never slips too far from the happy state of "clean enough." Routines are deliber-ately designed sets of steps, carried out at regular intervals, that automate household activities to make them easier.

You may be asking yourself, "What's the difference between a habit and a routine?" While a habit always has a routine at its core, routines don't always lend themselves to habit formation. Perhaps the activity occurs too infrequently to rise to the level of a habit. Other times, routines may involve more than one person, making it difficult to coordinate. While they aren't quite as reflexive as a good habit, routines serve the same purpose—to bundle and speed repetitive activities in everyday life.

Routines are particularly helpful in multiperson households, especially homes with children. Because routines spell out the sequence of steps, there's no need to stand over household members insisting that they first clear the glasses, then the plates, and then the serving dishes from the table. When clearing the table has become routine, everyone knows what's expected of them and understands how to proceed.

Crafting Robust Routines

The secret to crafting a routine is to think once and act many times. Setting out the steps required to do an activity and then listing them to guide the family the next time saves time and mental energy from that day forward. Also, by crafting your routines intentionally, you can refine them as needed. Planning a routine makes it possible to zero in on bottlenecks and problem areas and solve them, once and for all, in a way that slapdash daily attempts are unable to do.

The simplest and most durable routines are based on time. A routine that's triggered by the hour of the day, the day of the week, or the season of the year is easy to spot and easier to work with. To get organized fast, consider setting up these common routines:

- Morning wakeup
- Evening prebedtime
- Dinner preparation and cleanup
- Daily and weekly cleaning schedules

- Washing, drying, and folding clothing
- Shopping for groceries and storing food

SPEEDY SOLUTION

A tickler file tracks household routines easily. Write out routines on index cards and assign them a frequency. File cards behind calendar dividers in a file box. Each day, check for scheduled routines. When the routine has been completed, file the card behind the divider for the next scheduled interval. The job will come around again at the right time—all you have to do is check the file each day.

With routines that you don't execute often, such as seasonal yard chores, auto maintenance, or travel, the secret to success is a simple checklist.

File checklists in your control center notebook, or add them as reminders to an electronic calendar. For example, when it's time to put the yard to bed for the winter, you'll know where to find the list of chores that have to be done. Consider adding these ideas to your checklist-based routines:

- Changing out seasonal wardrobes
- Throwing a dinner party or birthday party
- Scheduling auto maintenance
- Performing spring-cleaning chores
- Decorating for the holidays
- Planning a picnic
- Adjusting clocks for Daylight Savings Time
- Completing a pretravel checklist

Create your own checklists to meet your specific needs, and visit OrganizedHome.com for free printable checklists to organize checklist-friendly activities like travel, yard sales, or party planning.

Automating Life's Activities

Finally, think beyond simple time- or checklist-based routines to find new ways to automate the activities of everyday life. Thinking outside the box to combine or consolidate everyday chores saves time and is the hallmark of an organized life.

Batching activities can be as simple as establishing an "errand day" each week. On that day, you'll handle all the week's errands, from grocery shopping, to banking, to dry cleaning. Because you're already out and about, each chore will take much less time than if you performed it singly.

Put the batching principle into action during the holidays to speed seasonal chores. Mix several batches of cookie dough on one weekend day, then bake all the cookies the next day to cut down on time and cleanup. Instead of weeding for a half-hour a day, recruit the family for a one-day yard-work session, and reward the crew with pizza. Whenever you can tick off multiple to-do items using the same tools and supplies, consider batching them to save time.

Simplifying activities means doing less and enjoying it more. Shave minutes off the morning tasks by doing away with bed-spreads in favor of quick-make duvets that can be straightened in seconds. Replace a trio of kitchen cleaning products with a multiuse solution that can clean every surface in the room to cut time spent cleaning. Think lean, mean ... and organized!

SPEEDY SOLUTION

In the old days, the milkman delivered dairy products to the doorstep. Today online subscription services offer the same timesaving solution for products as varied as dog food, vitamins, coffee, and printer cartridges. Schedule deliveries of consumables on a regular basis, and there'll be no more need to remember the milk.

Creating Activity Centers for an Organized Home

Like our souls, our surroundings need a center. Spaces support us best when they are organized around the activities we'll be doing in them, not according to label or location. To achieve this level of support, implement the concept of activity centers—dedicated places to carry out household functions.

For a model, look no further than a good preschool. Scan the room, and you'll see spaces allocated to every school-day pursuit. There's a dress-up corner, a sand table, and a gathering carpet for group activities like storybook reading. Each young pupil knows where to go to play, rest, or read. At day's end, little learners know where to go to put away blocks, toys, or dress-up costumes.

Putting the same concept to work in your home speeds life on every level. A well-stocked home office activity center means never having to leave the room to hunt for postage stamps. A gift-wrap station keeps everything you need to wrap and mail a birthday gift close at hand.

In the kitchen, centers work together to create an organized environment for cooking. Near the sink, you'll find a sink center, with strainers, cutting boards, peelers, and knives—everything you'll need to scrub and chop the evening vegetables. On the counter, an activity center focused on the oven contains measuring cups, an electric mixer, flour, and baking soda—everything you need to whip up a batch of muffins on a rainy day. At the stovetop, saucepans nest on nearby shelves, while spatulas, wooden spoons, and wire whisks stand ready to beat, fold, or blend.

Essentials of an Activity Center

To put the activity center concept to work, start by identifying the activity and making a list. Working room by room, list each activity that you carry out in the area. For example, a bedroom might have the following list:

- Sleeping
- Storing clothing
- Getting dressed
- Reading and watching television

For each activity, determine what you need to create a supportive center. Even if their locations overlap, each activity center will involve a different constellation of tools, materials, and supplies. The sleep center needs a night table, alarm clock, and bedside lamp; to watch television, you'll make use of the same night table and lamp, but add a remote control and a pair of eyeglasses for easy viewing.

Finally, assess the available storage options for each center. Place the most-used tools in the most accessible space, consigning things for occasional use to storage spaces where you have to stretch, bend, or reach. In the bedroom centers, extra blankets and a flashlight for emergencies find a home in an under-bed storage container, while used-daily items like the alarm clock and reading glasses take their place on the nightstand.

Get creative when establishing centers—efficient storage isn't limited to drawers and closets. Nondamaging adhesives anchor a small bin to hold the remote control on the wall next to the bed, or affix a hook to hang night clothes in the closet. An open basket next to the night table corrals books, reading glasses, and the television schedule. Think outside the dresser drawer to make your spaces work for you.

The Household Launch Pad

While any family's activity centers will be as individual as they are, most of us will want to create a household launch pad. Just as the space shuttle needs a structure to support it at liftoff, so do family members. A household launch pad is a dedicated place to manage the business of getting out the door each day.

A household launch pad is home to briefcases and diaper bags, backpacks and purses, and should be located near the entry door. Ensure that the location offers sufficient space for each household member to have a separate launch pad.

A dedicated section of counter space, low bookcases, or entryway tables are workable options for launch pad duty. Commercial solutions include specialized shelf units with hooks, low shelves, and multiple bins. Color-coded bins lined up on a shelf make a good choice for small children; add a charging station for electronic devices carried by teens and adults.

The household launch pad is home to all the stuff each family member needs to get out the door. For adults, it's the place where purses and briefcases land; for children, the launch pad corrals homework, library books, and lunchboxes. Parents can check the launch pad each day to find homework assignments and permission slips.

Head straight to the launch pad each afternoon to drop off paperwork, schoolbooks, lunch sacks, and ID badges. In the evening, check in at the launch pad to sign permission slips, wash out lunch containers, and complete the next day's paperwork. In the morning, the launch pad will blast the family forward again, fully supplied with the needs of the day.

Routines of an Organized Home

If you need proof of the organizing power of routines, look no further than day-to-day life at home. Domestic activities like cleaning, cooking, and washing clothes are made up of repetitive actions that lend themselves well to automation.

Housework is one arena where delay has a definite penalty. For instance, a drop of grape jelly spilled while making a sandwich can be wiped away quickly at the time but requires an all-out assault with a scrubbing pad if it's allowed to sit and harden. Also, setting aside 20 minutes a week to plan menus and make a shopping list heads off last-minute trips to the supermarket all week to find something for dinner. Well-crafted routines shorten the amount of time it takes to run a household, which means more playtime for everyone.

To get organized fast, get a realistic idea about what a clean and well-run house means to you, and then set up simple systems to keep it that way. In the kitchen, routines for meal planning, grocery shopping, and pantry management cut the time it takes to keep the family fed. Finally, establish a simple laundry routine to keep the clean clothes flowing.

Housecleaning and Home Maintenance

Cleaning is a dirty job, but somebody has to do it. For most of us, the bucket stops here. There are no maids or mommies around to clean up our messes. To keep our space in a reasonably comfortable condition, it's up to us to tackle the job.

Here's the good news: housecleaning is one of those areas where establishing routines pays off quickly and well. Fits-and-starts stabs at cleaning often compound the problem, merely relocating dirt from one place to another. Having a set of housecleaning routines can be the most efficient way to keep a "clean enough" house.

Why "clean enough," you ask? Because clean, like beauty, is in the eye of the beholder. Clean-freak friends may insist otherwise, but your standard for clean, like your clutter tolerance and your time-management style, is an individual assessment. To create effective cleaning routines, get to know where your household lies (or should lie) on the cleaning scale.

Family composition and personal preferences dictate the parameters of what means "clean" to any given household. Young adult roommates can have fairly carefree standards, while a family with floor-crawling infants will likely have a much more rigorous definition. To clean a house fast, make sure you're aiming at the right target for your household; set a standard for clean that makes sense to you and your family.

Your next step is to negotiate that standard with the entire household. Other family members may have a different idea of what "clean" should mean and their own ideas about how best to get there. To set up a routine everyone can live with, the whole family needs to be on board.

ROAD HAZARD

"My way or the highway" mindsets complicate housekeeping
negotiations. Instead, play to their strengths. Family
members with higher standards can be responsible for areas
about which they feel more strongly, like bathrooms. Those
with more casual preferences can take on chores with less
potential for variance in performance, such as vacuuming or
taking out the trash.

Daily

Daily housekeeping routines are all about maintenance. Taking
small cleaning steps each day keeps soil from building up and
holds clutter at bay. Follow daily routines faithfully, and you'll
win 80 percent of the battle of keeping a clean house.

A simple morning routine sees the family out the door and leaves
behind a clean and organized home. A sample morning routine
can include items like these:

- Make beds or straighten duvets and pillows.
- Spritz shower walls with daily shower cleaner after
  showering.
- Wipe the bathroom sink, toilet seat, and toilet rim
  before you leave the room.
- Dry and fold one load of laundry.
- Empty the dishwasher and load the dirty breakfast
  dishes.
- Take out the trash on your way out the door.

In the evening, take time to tidy up after the day's activities and
to set the stage for the following day. An evening routine might
include items like these:

- Sort mail into recycling bin and action files.
- Wash one load of laundry.

- Wipe down kitchen counters and sinks.
- Run the dishwasher.
- Set the table for breakfast.
- Sweep and/or damp-mop the kitchen floor.
- Put away personal belongings and clean laundry.

Weekly

Weekly cleaning activities work to banish built-up dust, tackle deposited soil, and return floors to an acceptable state of clean. Add items like these to your weekly cleaning list:

- Vacuum carpets and hard-surface floors.
- Dust furniture, fixtures, and artwork.
- Iron clothing.
- Clean toilet bowls, rims, and seat.
- Clean bathroom mirrors.
- Scrub bathroom sinks and counters.
- Clean bathroom floors.
- Clean out the refrigerator and wipe down shelves.
- Scrub and disinfect the kitchen sink.
- Wash the kitchen floor.

Monthly

Once-a-month cleaning routines tackle the tough stuff and get to the bottom of stubborn grime with deep-cleaning chores. Depending on the season of the year, your monthly routine may include tasks such as these:

- Wash interior windows.
- Vacuum upholstery and drapes.
- Dust baseboards.

- Spot-clean walls.
- Dust ceiling fans.
- Change furnace filters.

SPEEDY SOLUTION

Spring-cleaning is a holdover from a time when homes were heated by wood or coal, which left residue on walls and furniture. Modern households may not need to conduct a traditional spring clean; once-a-year fall cleaning may be enough!

Seasonal

As the seasons change, so do household cleaning needs. Spring cleaning removes dust and dirt that's accumulated in a winter-tight house, while fall cleaning routs out the dusty remains of summer. Seasonal cleaning routines might include these:

- Wash exterior windows.
- Clean light fixtures and light-diffusing bowls.
- Wash walls and baseboards.
- Steam-clean carpets.
- Launder or dry-clean window treatments.
- Vacuum underneath and behind furniture.

With cleaning, as with cars, your mileage may vary. A two-career couple may find that they can get away with biweekly cleaning sessions, while an at-home parent of preschool children may need to add many more chores to daily cleaning routines. Adjust your routines to suit your own circumstances, for a clean and organized home.

Managing Meals and Menus

It's 5 o'clock—do you know where your dinner is? Judging by the crowds in the supermarket, many families do not! Adopting time-saving routines for menu planning, grocery shopping, and food storage can save hours of time, hundreds of dollars, and an ocean of end-of-day stress.

Menu- and Meal-Planning Basics

Say the words "menu plan," and objections pop up all over. "It takes too much time!" "How do I know what we're going to want to eat three days from now?" "I like to see what's fresh at the store each day." Often the idea of making a simple list of meals to be served in the household over the next week seems daunting, so you put it off. The result is four days of drive-thru dinners that pump up the blood pressure or time-consuming daily trips to the supermarket.

Compared to joining the after-work lines at the grocery store, making a menu plan is a walk in the park. Start small with a weekly dinner plan. Grab your calendar and a sheet of paper, or print a free weekly menu planner from OrganizedHome.com. Look over the week ahead and make a quick list of what the household will eat each night for dinner. List entrée, side dishes, drinks, and dessert for each day's evening meal, and you're done!

Keep your calendar in mind as you plan. An evening spent shuttling the soccer team is no time to try a complicated new recipe, so save recreational cooking for free weekend evenings. Match quick-fix entrées to busy nights, or put the slow cooker into play to have dinner waiting when you arrive home from the soccer field.

Your next step is to check your pantry. Start a shopping list, noting any items you'll need to buy to prepare the meals on your menu plan. Scanning the food ads in the newspaper or online, plan shopping trips to take advantage of sales.

SPEEDY SOLUTION

For the fastest menu plan, use a monthly calendar and packet of small sticky notes. Write dinner menus on the sticky notes and paste them to the relevant date. Need to rearrange meals? Swap the sticky notes. Next week, repost favorite meals and stow the extra notes on the back of the calendar for later use.

Finally, post your menu plan publicly. Each morning, check the list. Will you need to remove items from the freezer or start the slow cooker before you leave? Get the jump on dinner in the morning to cut stress at the end of the day.

After you've made weekly menu plans for a few weeks, you'll see some themes begin to appear in your planning. You'll notice that supermarket sales appear in regular rotation, and that the family's week-by-week activities have a predictable rhythm. Take advantage of these menu-planning cycles to save time and money.

For example, supermarket specials operate on regular six- to eight-week sale cycles. Knowing that boneless chicken breasts will be offered at a good price about every six weeks helps you make a menu plan that takes advantage of this savings cycle. Grilled chicken, chicken enchiladas, and a hearty chicken soup could all make the menu that week.

As another example, you may notice that certain weeks each month have a faster—or slower—pace of activities. Busy weeks, with extra evening meetings or sports practices, will call for quick-fix dinner plans; more relaxed weeks signal the time to plan more elaborate dinners. Recycling menu plans to meet these cyclical challenges simplifies shopping and cooking chores.

Once you've conquered the dinner hour, consider expanding menu-planning efforts. A rotating weekly breakfast plan standardizes the shopping list as well and fights the daily cold cereal habit. Expanding menu planning from a week to a month at a time taps the savings offered by bulk buying at the supermarket or warehouse clubs.

Shopping Tips

When you step into your local market, you're entering a battleground for your time and money. Savvy retailers know that grocery spending increases the longer you're in the store, so they've designed store layouts to delay you as long as possible. The added distractions of on-site bakeries and coffee shops, end-of-aisle displays, and confusing multiple pricing options make it easy to lose track of time and your budget while shopping.

Save your valuable time and money by fighting back with these tips for speedy, efficient shopping:

1. **Use a shopping list.** Waiting to decide what you need until you're at the store makes you an easy target for budget-busting impulse buys. Make a shopping list from the comfort of home, and don't deviate from it. No list entry, no dice—and no DVDs, candy bars, or cut flowers, either.

2. **Shop alone.** Family members of all ages bring built-in distractions and their own agendas to the process of shopping. When you can, fly solo. You'll escape from the premises faster and cheaper.

3. **Shop less often.** Quick trips to the supermarket are out-sized time wasters. Use a shopping list and a menu plan to get in there once, get what you need, and get out the door … and stay out!

Keeping Order in the Pantry

You've planned your meals and shopped for them efficiently, so don't quit now! The next step to kitchen efficiency is to store food properly to preserve freshness and flavor. Try these simple steps to manage pantry and food storage:

- Wash and store produce directly after you buy it.
- Repackage meat or poultry into meal-size portions.
- Store perishable items in the coldest spots in the refrigerator.
- Rotate pantry products, adding new items to the back of the shelf.
- Seal open packages of rice or pasta with zipper-lock food-storage bags.
- Label and date frozen foods, and package them to prevent freezer burn.
- Check stored vegetables regularly for sprouting or decay.

ROAD HAZARD

Television programs devoted to "extreme couponing" are fun to watch, but be careful! Too often, forays into couponing lead to cluttered pantries and food waste. Limit coupon use to products your household actually uses, and in quantities that make sure you'll use them up. A bargain's no bargain if it just gets thrown away.

Wardrobe Planning and Clothing Care

Bringing order to clothes closets and keeping laundry chores under control brings real-time payoff to a busy household. Wardrobe planning cuts scatter-shot shopping trips and keeps spending in check; conquering chaos in the laundry room keeps the clean clothes flowing. No more early-morning basket-diving sessions in search of clean underwear!

Planning Family Wardrobes

Shopping for clothes as the spirit moves you can be a lot of fun, but it's no way to build a working wardrobe. Crafting an integrated collection of clothes that work together takes a plan; the goal is to get you out the door each morning, ready for any event or activity that will come your way.

Take charge of family wardrobes with this simple wardrobe planning routine:

1. **Declutter existing clothing.** Sort crammed drawers, tossing stained, outworn, or outgrown items as you go. In the closet, quickly sort items by type—shirts, pants, dresses, or skirts—and hang like items together. Toss worn-out or out-of-style items into a donation box.

2. **Evaluate clothing needs.** List the types of clothing necessary for your lifestyle, be it work clothes, dressy outfits, and casual or fitness wear. Compare your decluttered closet to your list. Will you need to add or replace garments? If so, start a shopping list.

3. **Play matchmaker with the survivors.** Try on and assemble outfits for each clothing type you identified in the last step. Be creative! Mix and match to make the most of what you have. If you need to fill in an outfit, make a note of it on the shopping list.

4. **Update wardrobes seasonally.** When packing away seasonal clothing, declutter as you go; it's easier to toss worn garments than to store them. As you bring seasonal clothing out for use, review your list of clothing needs and assemble outfits as you unpack. Keep a shopping list handy for any fill-in items and for ideas for new purchases to bring your wardrobe up-to-date.

Creating a Laundry Activity Center

Cut the crazy out of laundry day by creating a laundry activity center in your home to speed washing chores. If your household includes a washer and dryer, they'll anchor your center for efficient clothing care. For families who launder clothing off-site, a mobile laundry center will cut time and expense at the laundromat and make it easier to transport clothing and supplies.

Too often, laundry areas lack sufficient storage and space to support the activity. Examine your household laundry area with an eye for function. Is there a place to store detergent, fabric softener, and stain-removal supplies? A slender rolling cart creates a good home for laundry products if it can be placed between the washer and dryer.

Next, look at your walls. Do you have a place to hang just-dried clothing? Mount a clothing rod on an adjacent wall to snap the wrinkles out of shirts, dresses, and jeans. If folding space is hard to come by, consider a drop-down shelf. It will help you smooth and fold sheets and T-shirts, and can be folded up and out of the way when it's not in use.

If you travel to a laundromat to wash your clothing, put the same principle to work, but make your activity center portable. Stock a bucket or cleaning tote with laundry products for easy transport. Presort dirty laundry into separate laundry bags, one per load. Set aside small bills or stockpile change to make it easy to fire up the washers and dryers. A nested stack of laundry baskets lets you sort freshly cleaned clothing as you fold it. At home, have family members grab their basket and go!

Crafting Clothing-Care Routines

With your laundry activity center stocked and ready, it's time to craft a get-it-done laundry routine. Your family size will dictate whether you need to do laundry daily, weekly, or a couple times a month. Create a schedule that is frequent enough to keep the clean clothes coming without resorting to partial loads.

A sample laundry routine might look like this:

- Once a week, collect dirty laundry and sort it into a divided laundry hamper.
- Run one load of laundry each morning, after the family showers.
- Dry and fold one load of laundry each evening, sorting folded clothes into color-coded laundry baskets.
- Before bed, put away clean laundry and return baskets to the laundry area.

Crafting Organized Spaces

How well is your home working for you? Try a little test. Ask yourself how much time it would take to find an immunization record, hang a picture, replace the batteries in a remote control, or locate a spare house key. That long? Then it's time to get organized!

In this chapter, you'll develop a plan to fine-tune storage and surroundings and create organized spaces for each activity in the home. Tapping the principle of contained clutter, we'll look at ways to keep your stuff accessible yet under control. We'll get creative with storage options and explore ways to make peace with multiuse areas.

Assigning Household Real Estate

On the day you moved into your home, with boxes stacked high and your possessions strewn about, the goal was likely to get items put away as quickly as possible. Years later, these items may still be squatting in the place where they landed way back then, efficient or not.

For an organized home, you need to assign space in a deliberate and conscious manner. Setting up supportive spaces takes a bit of thought and may require rethinking ideas about storage. A well-thought-out plan to allocate household real estate puts your space to work for you so that it functions efficiently.

To get started, you'll need to know:

- What activities each space hosts
- What items and equipment are needed
- What storage options are available

To craft a household storage plan, grab a notebook and take a walk around the house. Working room by room, quickly write down each activity that is carried out in that space.

Some rooms, such as bathrooms, have a single function—personal care. Other rooms, like family rooms, have a much longer list, such as watching television, reading, visiting with family and friends, playing with children, listening to music, and playing video games.

For each activity on your list, note the items you need to carry it out. For example, in the bathroom, personal care requires supplies such as shampoo, equipment such as electric razors or hair dryers, and items such as towels and bath mats.

Next, list available storage in each area. The bathroom has a towel rack, an under-sink cabinet, and a set of drawers, along with some space on the countertop. Evaluate whether you need to add more storage options. Note the places stuff currently overflows to get a feel for necessary improvements.

Finally, take a look at what doesn't belong in the space. Out-of-place items steal space from the hard-working stuff you need to get the job done. These interlopers have to be relocated to a more appropriate home.

ROAD HAZARD

When assessing available storage, decorations can be your downfall. Pretty as they are, decorative items can be space hogs, crowding out access to the things you really need. To stay organized, send them to the back of the line. Add decorative items only after needed tools and supplies have been assigned a home where they need to be.

With an idea of what you have to work with, it's time to get creative with how you can arrange the items you need to make this space work for you.

Location, Location, Location

When it comes to buying a house, real estate agents have a simple saying: "Location, location, location!" Just as your home's value is largely dependent on how accessible it is to shopping, recreation, and work, storage spaces operate by the same principle—they are more or less desirable depending on where they're located. Put this principle to work to store your stuff in an organized way.

Give storage spaces a letter grade to guide how you'll use them. A storage spaces live life front and center: you can reach them without bending, stretching, or moving from the spot you're working. In a bathroom, the counter and top drawer offer the most accessible storage areas, so reserve them for items used frequently, like hand soap, toothbrushes, and a razor.

Accessing B storage zones takes a little more work. If you have to bend over to open a drawer or stretch to reach an upper shelf, you've reached the B storage category. Stow things used often but not daily—like curling irons, manicure tools, or beard trimmers—in these less convenient zones.

C spaces are hard-to-reach locations reserved for items you don't use very often. The far back of the cabinet under the sink qualifies as a C zone. Since you need to squat to reach this space, it's the place to store once-in-a-blue-moon items like hair-coloring supplies and jewelry cleaner.

When making your storage plan, map out A, B, and C spaces for storing items according to frequency of use. Think daily, weekly, and monthly to match tools and equipment to the right storage space.

Hot Zones and Black Holes

Two other types of storage categories can be spotted in most homes: hot zones and black holes. Anchoring opposite ends of the space-efficiency spectrum, these special-case areas represent extremes of household storage. Hot zones are so convenient that they're oversubscribed; black holes are so hard to reach that they're nearly impossible to use.

Hot zones are created when worlds collide; they spring up where overlapping storage needs compete for a single space. The kitchen counter nearest the living area frequently takes on a hot zone identity, with piles of mail, lunchboxes, and a cellphone charger all laying claim to the space.

Cope with hot zones by sorting out the different functions that compete for space and by finding space for those activities elsewhere. To reclaim the kitchen counter for cooking, you'll need to set up a family launch pad to corral lunchboxes and cellphones, and reroute the mail to an action file in the home office.

Once you've identified a hot zone, it's a signal to be vigilant. These areas draw clutter like polyester attracts cat hair! To keep them free from clutter buildup, add a "hot zone sweep" to daily routines.

Black holes, on the other hand, are storage areas that have some quirk or shortcoming that makes them difficult to use. For example, in a narrow coat closet, a high shelf placed above the level of the door opening offers a lot of potential storage space but can be reached only through the narrow slot between shelf and wall.

In a kitchen, black hole space arises in L-shaped cabinet areas. Their corner configuration means you have to bury yourself up to the hips in the cabinet to reach items stored there.

Treat black holes as independent storage areas unrelated to where they happen to be located. Make them home to seldom-used items that can fit in the oddly configured space. For that closet with the narrow opening, store pillows and cushions in it, since they can be compressed to fit through. The dark recesses of the kitchen black hole make a good home for bulky seasonal items like the turkey roaster and Thanksgiving serving platters. Diving in to retrieve them will become another holiday tradition!

SPEEDY SOLUTION

Make it easier to put things away than it is to get them out. Shifting the effort to the front end of the transaction puts human nature to work for you.

Clever Containment Strategies

No matter how spacious a house, it's unlikely you'll be able to stow everything you own behind closed doors. Find a solution with containment strategies: out-in-the-open methods to keep your stuff stored in view but within bounds.

Containment strategies are especially useful for those of "the piler" persuasion. Stuff stays where you can see it without being permitted to sprawl, yet any visual hint of a pile is overcome by the restrictions created by the container. It's a win-win!

For filers, containment strategies create intermediate staging areas to hold items in transit to their forever home. When bringing in the mail, toss new magazines into a shallow basket near the reading chair; after they've been thumbed through, they can be sorted into separate bookcase files for future reference.

Try these containment solutions to corral clutter around the house:

- Stack newspapers in a shallow basket beneath an end table or coffee table.
- Stand CDs, DVDs, and video games title side up in a plastic organizer bin.
- Manage magazine clutter with wall-mounted racks to hold current issues.
- Keep pens and pencils at the ready in a cheerful coffee mug near the phone.
- Keep craft supplies close at hand underneath a worktable in a rolling drawer cart.
- Store bulky bedding, sports equipment, or toys in footlockers and trunks.
- Corral bottles of condiments in a small basket to speed sandwich making.
- Display stuffed animals in wall-mounted baskets in a child's room.
- Use pretty boxes with a lid to organize ongoing craft projects.
- Organize paper on the shelves of a hanging canvas sweater caddy.

Since there will be a constant in-and-out aspect to clutter containment, make it easy to add or remove contents. Open or easily accessible containers work best to contain clutter.

Storage Options High to Low

To discover a storage bonanza around the house, look around from high to low. Spaces on top of cabinets, beneath furniture, or on empty walls or doors offer unexplored options for household storage.

The World Beneath

Untapped storage space lives all around you, hiding beneath the furniture. While under-bed storage is a commonly used solution, it's also possible to take advantage of free space beneath sofas, end tables, and bookcases to house your stuff.

Under the bed, sweep the dust bunnies aside to make room for long, shallow storage bins or self-contained storage drawers. Use bed risers and an extra-deep bed skirt to increase space available beneath the bed. Keep under-bed items contained in organizer bins to keep dust out and make stored items easy to retrieve.

Good candidates for under-bed storage include gift wrap, craft supplies and bed linens. Space-saving vacuum storage bags make it possible to slide extra pillows and puffy comforters into under-bed space. More unusual uses of this space include storage for folding banquet tables, table leaves, and the ironing board.

Tap shallower spaces, such as those beneath end tables or sofas, to store extra picture frames or seasonal wall art. Clear acrylic picture frames come in sizes to fit any space and slide neatly beneath an office desk or bookcase. Use them to hold office supplies, computer cables, or oversize printer paper. Add a label to make it easy to spot the contents under the desk.

SPEEDY SOLUTION

Luggage does double duty as storage for out-of-season clothing. Slide it beneath the bed or stack filled suitcases in an attic corner. Clothing stays clean and dust free in the off season, and is easy to swap out when the weather changes.

Look Up High

Kitchen cabinets often stop short of the ceiling, creating a natural storage space for seldom-used small appliances and oversize serving dishes. One caveat: be prepared to cope with the airborne greasy film generated by cooking. Restrict cabinet-top storage to items that can be easily washed to remove it.

Try the bowl trick to maximize storage in high spaces. Fill a decorative bowl with small items like table games or decks of playing cards. Placed on a shelf above eye level, the bowl's contents are hidden yet accessible.

In the computer area or entertainment center, set up electronic devices such as network routers and digital antennas on the top shelves of high bookcases. The bookcase screens the devices (and their clutter of cords) from view, while the high-up location enhances signal reception and Wi-Fi coverage. In children's bedrooms, mount a high shelf on one, some, or all of the walls around the room. Doll collections, stuffed animals, and board games can live there happily and free up play space in the center of the room.

On the Walls

The empty space on walls offers potential storage. In the garage, screw simple U- or L-brackets into adjoining studs to hold window screens, replacement furnace filters, or scrap lumber flat against the wall. Near the workbench, pegboards and tool racks provide easy hanging options for tools and garden equipment.

Inside the house, wall-mounted file holders put mail sorting on the fast track or hold action files for household paperwork. Modular storage systems allow you to mix and match bulletin boards, whiteboards, bins, and hooks to create a family launch pad or home office communications center. Shallow cupboards, set into walls between framing studs, make good homes for prescription drugs, spices, or small tools.

Freestanding floor-to-ceiling solutions tap usable vertical space in unusual areas. Specialty bike racks allow apartment dwellers to safeguard and stack their wheels without marring the walls. In the shower, tension pole caddies make use of corners to keep soap and shampoo and conditioner bottles off the floor. A toilet topper shelf unit creates storage space over the commode.

Double-Duty Doors

The backs of closet and cabinet doors offer instant A-category storage when enhanced with hooks, racks, or over-the-door storage organizers.

Walking the dog will be a pleasure when the leash, harness, and cleanup kit hang ready to go on a rack mounted on the back door. An over-door ironing center keeps the ironing board, iron, and spray starch close at hand in the laundry area.

Another way to maximize a door storage area is to harness the hinges. Specialty products designed to attach to door hinges offer storage space for flat items like towels and folded trousers, allowing you to reclaim unused space behind the open door.

Adhesive hooks and hangers offer damage-free storage solutions to organize your space. Products such as 3M-brand Command hanging strips install quickly and can be removed cleanly, without nail holes or damage to paint. Use them to mount hooks, shelves, or bins where you need them.

Organizing Multiuse Spaces

When two or more activities share one space, it's important that each activity be self-contained. Nobody wants to throw a dinner party with the sewing machine taking the place at the head of the table. To craft a workable solution, you need to set up spaces that you can close off when the activity is not in play.

Simple solutions for multiuse spaces include visual dividers such as screens. Give the sewing machine a home on a small corner table, and add a rolling organizer cart to store scissors, pattern pieces, and sewing tools. When not in use, screen the sewing corner from view with a folding shoji screen or ceiling-mounted curtain.

A closet with folding doors can anchor an activity center in a multiuse area as well. To incorporate a mailing center into the guest room, mount a desk-level shelf in the closet to provide workspace for wrapping and addressing packages. Flattened boxes can be stacked and stashed under the bed, while wares to be sent are stored on closet shelves. With the door closed, houseguests will never suspect that they're sleeping in the office of an eBay auctioneer!

In multiuse rooms, compartmentalization is the secret to storage success. Resist the urge to sweep a half-finished sewing project into a drawer in the dining room breakfront when it's time to set the table. Muddling storage spaces makes it more difficult to swap activities out when necessary.

Instead, keep storage separate. Portable totes, lidded plastic storage containers, and open storage solutions such as restaurant bus bins make it easier to change the room's function from one activity to the other. For even faster transformations, use storage on wheels. Rolling carts and wheeled crates slide under desk areas and make quick work of camouflaging an activity area.

Organized Spaces, Room by Room

Around the house, it's time to start organizing space, stuff, and storage in every room. From the kitchen to the family room, these household areas feature different constellations of activities and storage options. Creating custom solutions room by room moves us closer to the goal of an organized life.

In this chapter, we dive into kitchen activity centers and round up the best ideas for storage in the kitchen and pantry. In the bedroom and bathroom, our focus is on creating a calm oasis for rest and renewal. Finally, in shared living spaces like the family room, we'll work to accommodate competing claims for space and storage to create a welcoming multiuse room.

Organizing Kitchen and Food-Storage Areas

If there's ever a place where activities clash, it's the kitchen! Because the kitchen is the heart of the home, it attracts family members and the possessions in their wake. Papers pile up, school assignments sprawl out, and scattered shoes and jackets clamor to join the fun. To bring order to the kitchen, begin by identifying and relocating activities best carried out elsewhere. Setting up family launch pads and creating a life-management center for planning and paperwork diverts the flood of paper and possessions to more appropriate locations.

Setting Up Kitchen Activity Centers

Visualizing the kitchen in terms of activity centers helps organize the space efficiently. Most kitchens contain these activity centers:

- Stovetop, for cooking
- Oven, for baking
- Sink, for preparing food and washing dishes
- Refrigerator/freezer, for cold storage
- Pantry, for room-temperature storage

Kitchen activity centers overlap to a greater or lesser degree, depending on the size of your kitchen. For instance, a single drawer may be part of two or even three activity centers.

At the *stovetop*, the activity center zeroes in on the space in, on, and immediately around the stove. Store pots and pans, spoons and ladles, potholders, and often-used supplies like salt and pepper so you can reach them without having to move away from the stove.

The *oven* activity center is home to roasting and baking. Oven-safe dishes, cookie sheets, cake pans, measuring spoons, and mixing bowls must be stored nearby. The oven activity center also needs easy access to baking supplies like flour and cooking spray, small appliances such as a mixer, and specialty tools like the rolling pin.

Food is prepared and dishes are washed at the *sink* activity center. Nearby, you'll want to store strainers, cutting boards, vegetable brushes, and cutlery. A trashcan and composting bin should be located in a convenient spot to handle food refuse. Under the sink, keep dishwasher detergent, scrubbing sponges, and specialty cleaners for silver or brass close at hand for easy cleanup.

In the *refrigerator/freezer*, family members hunt for food, chilled drinks, and ice cubes. Store drinking glasses nearby for beverage service, and simplify storing leftovers by keeping plastic wrap, freezer storage bags, and disposable containers near the refrigerator.

The *pantry* activity center is home to long-term food storage. Canned goods, beans and pasta, and cereal products share this space with backup supplies of cooking oil, bottled dressings and sauces, and boxed mixes.

SPEEDY SOLUTION

Kitchen counter space is far too valuable to act as a catchall for items that belong elsewhere. Set up a lost-and-found box near the kitchen. Sweep wandering items off the counters and into the box, and refer owners to the lost-and-found box to retrieve missing possessions.

Stand back in your kitchen and map out the location of each activity center. The cabinet nearest the sink, along with a nearby drawer, marks the boundaries of the sink area. Cabinets beneath a cooktop or next to the range can be assigned to the stovetop center. Mapping out activity centers in this way brings a natural order to the kitchen.

Assign kitchen tools and implements to their appropriate center. The potato peeler and vegetable knife live near the sink center, while muffin tins and cake pans hang out with the crowd near the oven. Whether doing the dishes or preparing a snack, your goal is to have everything you need for that activity as close at hand as possible.

Creative Kitchen Organization Ideas

Because it hosts so many different activities, the kitchen takes all the organizing power you can muster. To get organized in the kitchen, check out this potpourri of tips:

- Keep the kitchen honed to items you need and use frequently. Find storage for oversize cooking pans, seasonal tools, and extra dishes outside the hard-working everyday kitchen area.

- To make the best use of space in the back of cabinets, install pullout drawers in lower cabinet areas. Running on rails, they bring cabinet contents to you! Install a pullout for the trashcan, too, if you store it beneath the sink. For easier recycling, double-can pullouts allow you to sort out recyclables as you toss the trash.

- Under the kitchen sink, lay claim to the murky space beneath the garbage disposer with an oversize lazy Susan. A quick spin brings stored cleaning products out from the back and into the light of day.

- Customize shelf heights to maximize storage potential in cabinets or pantry. Begin by stocking cabinets at the bottom, setting each shelf to an appropriate height for the items it will hold. To add extra shelves to the cabinet, have the lumberyard trim ready-made shelves to the sizes you'll need.

- When tall items share a shelf with shorter ones, adding a freestanding wire shelf organizer allows you to double-stack the little guys, leaving the long fellows to stand tall on the rest of the shelf.

- Vertical storage works well for cookie sheets, cutting boards, and serving trays. To protect these items, install simple spring tension rods to subdivide vertical space, or look for premade organizers to create vertical cubbies for slender pans.

- Cabinet-door storage units turn empty space into prime real estate. Use them to organize plastic wrap, food-storage bags, spice jars, and pan lids. Full-size door organizers create bonus pantry space on the back of the door.

ROAD HAZARD

Wood and water don't mix; don't store sponges, scrubbing brushes, or hand towels where they can touch cabinet surfaces. Draping a hand towel over an under-sink cabinet door attracts moisture that will damage the wood finish. Find the towel a home on a towel rack to preserve your kitchen's beauty.

- If small children live in your household, store plastic cups, cereal bowls, and cartoon character plates in a low, easy-to-reach location. Having access to their own stuff encourages children to help set the table and put away clean dishes.

- When selecting small appliances, look for models that can be mounted underneath the cabinet. Storing items like coffee makers and can openers underneath upper cabinets keeps them close at hand and off the kitchen counter.

- Be selective about the array of accessories that come packaged with small appliances. If you haven't used an accessory in a month or two, you never will; release it to make space in the kitchen.

- Don't be afraid to break up sets. Just because dishes come with a certain number of place settings to the box doesn't mean you can't limit stacks of plates to the number you use regularly. Remove extras to an exterior storage area to keep the kitchen lean and mean.

- Stick with see-through solutions for kitchen storage. Clear food-storage containers make it easy to tell whether there's cereal or spaghetti inside; see-through plastic food-storage bags protect open packages of food without obscuring their identities.

- Where needed, use drawer dividers to mark the informal boundary between kitchen activity centers. The sink area's vegetable brush and can opener are stored on one side of a shared drawer; measuring cups and the rolling pin spread out on the other.

- Don't overfill drawers. Tempting as it is to cram it all in there, be sure you can see each item in the drawer at a glance. Drawer dividers create compartments to keep kitchen tools separated and easy to find.

- Free up scarce drawer space by displaying pretty wooden spoons, spatulas, and whisks upright in a small canister. While cooking, you can reach them easily, and they add a note of gourmet charm to the kitchen.

- Store flatware in a divided basket or picnic tote. Choose a unit with a sturdy handle so you can easily move the silverware from dishwasher, to counter, to tabletop.

- Nondamaging adhesive hooks offer versatile solutions for any kitchen. Apply one near the oven to hang potholders for ready use. An adhesive clip corrals coupons and the weekly shopping list, ready to grab and go.

- Magnetic knife strips store knives and cutlery safely and conveniently. Hang them inside a cabinet door, out of reach of children. When knives aren't bumping about in the drawer, they'll avoid nicks and knocks that dull their edges and will stay sharp longer.

SPEEDY SOLUTION

Encourage family members to pitch in and help by labeling the edge of kitchen shelves with the names of items to be placed there. Electronic label makers create adhesive labels that are easy to read and slim enough to fit shelf edges.

Bringing Order to Bed and Bath Areas

At their best, bedrooms and bathrooms are the ultimate retreat from a chaotic world. Too often, however, bedrooms become crowded repositories of refugee items from the rest of the house; and bathrooms become overstuffed storage areas due to lack of space, creating an uninviting environment for personal care.

To start each new day with a spring in your step, it's time to restore peace and order to the most private areas of your home. Try these ideas to cut the clutter and calm the chaos in bedroom and bath.

Creating Blissful Bedrooms

Sleep therapists (and marriage counselors!) tell us that bedrooms work best when restricted to a single task: rest. Looking around, however, you wouldn't know it. In one corner, a dusty treadmill is draped with geologic layers of discarded clothing. Along the wall, storage boxes tumble in unsteady stacks, while an unfinished craft project spills over the top of a portable table.

Get organized in the bedroom by listing activities you'd like to pursue there, keeping in mind the goal of a restful and supportive space. As you ponder potential bedroom activity centers, evaluate the objects currently in the room with a critical eye. Dust on the treadmill is evidence of wishful thinking, not actual exercise!

Clearing out the items that don't belong in the room is the next order of business. Use the STOP clutter method discussed in Chapter 3 to assess and reroute wayward stuff and free your bedroom space.

Finally, revamp bedroom storage areas and tap new ones with these tips:

- Beneath the bed lies a treasure trove of bedroom storage space. Make good use of it to store folded sweaters, extra blankets, or out-of-season clothing. Long, shallow plastic organizers designed for under-bed storage slide out easily, while their lids protect contents from dust. Slip an emergency kit beneath the bed, too, to keep a flashlight, extra batteries, emergency radio, and fire escape close by.

- Grandma knew what she was doing when she added a cedar chest to the foot of her bed! Pillows and blankets fill the space nicely, while the closed chest adds extra seating.

- On the bedside table, create an overnight charging center for cellphones and tablet computers. Plug charger bases in a multioutlet surge protector, and use adhesive cable loops to position charger tips atop the table. Your cellphone will wake as refreshed as you are!

- Put the back of the bedroom and closet doors to good use. Over-the-door hooks hold bathrobes and pajamas, while a drawstring bag collects clothing on the way to the dry cleaner. Stow scarves, hats, and accessories in the pockets of an over-the-door shoe bag.

Bathrooms That Work for You

It's hard to pull together a polished look each morning if you're hindered by clutter and chaos in the bathroom. Streamline your center for personal care with these ideas for an organized bathroom:

- When bathroom storage space is limited, designate a remote storage area as a bathroom pantry. Consign extra bottles of mouthwash, bulk packs of toilet tissue, and extra packages of cotton swabs to storage elsewhere, restricting bathroom storage to just what you need for immediate use.

- Small shelves or specialty wall mounts provide a good home for personal care items and appliances used daily, while keeping them off the bathroom counter.

- Store towels in the bathroom, close to where they are used. Install towel bars above or below existing towel bars, to multiply available towel storage. A basket of rolled towels provides extra storage and a decorative touch. If you have no room on the floor, stack rolled towels on a narrow shelf for a colorful accent.

- In the shower, make space for shampoo, conditioner, and shower gel with a hanging shower caddy or tension-pole shower organizer, or take a tip from the gym and install wall-mounted dispensers. Alternately, place personal shower items in small plastic baskets to tote supplies in and out of the shower quickly.

 ROAD HAZARD

Just because we call it a medicine chest doesn't mean medicine should be stored there. Heat and humidity can adversely affect medications and nutritional supplements. Instead, store these products in a cool, dry location—such as the linen closet—to protect their potency.

Creating Orderly Family Rooms

Family rooms are the center of household life, and chances are that's where you'll find the people you love, trailing their stuff behind them. Factor in "entertainment clutter" in the form of electronic devices, reading material, and board games, and it's clear that keeping the family room inviting and orderly represents a special challenge.

Rise to the occasion by negotiating appropriate activities, stripping down the area to basics, and finding creative storage solutions.

Activity Centers for Shared Spaces

Ask an average family what goes on in the family room, and the answers will be all over the map. Common activities for this shared space can include these:

- Watching television and movies
- Working on the computer
- Playing video games
- Eating snacks
- Doing homework
- Reading books and periodicals

Evaluate what's on the activity center list for your family room, and then clear the decks by identifying and relocating activities that don't belong in this shared space. Move the computer station to the home office area or household command center to free up space and storage. If snacking is a problem, negotiate a "no food" policy; while unpopular, it can go a long way toward improving the atmosphere of the family room.

Décor, too, needs to adapt to the public purpose of the area. Simplify decorating and scale back on designer touches. Use the walls to display photos and knick-knacks, or restrict them to a single shelf; this keeps coffee tables and end tables clutter free.

When you're stripping surroundings for family room action, don't neglect media items. Review movie and audio collections for duplicate titles. Do you need to have VHS, DVD, and Blu-ray editions of the same movie? Can you substitute a video-by-mail subscription or a streaming option for an owned library of favorite movies?

In the same vein, evaluate media platforms with an eye to making room in the entertainment center. If your Blu-ray player is backward compatible, there's no need to retain the old DVD player, and still less need to hold on to an antique VHS system. Move music collections to a digital format and release physical CD disks and cases. Keep the fun and cull the stuff to make best use of shared space.

SPEEDY SOLUTION

Magazine files have come a long way from their drab office-supply-store beginnings. Vivid colors and designer patterns bring a decorating spark to bookcases; inside, they keep magazine collections, torn-out articles, or recipes at your fingertips.

Storage Ideas for Entertainment, Books, and Music

The principle of clutter containment goes a long way toward cutting down on chaos in the family room. Use baskets to corral remotes and game controllers, store magazines in magazine racks, and stack newspapers in shallow baskets on shelves or under tables. Containing entertainment clutter will keep what you need where you need it.

Do DVDs and video game disks abandon their cases to hang out in dusty corners of the family room? Bow to the inevitable and protect your digital investment; store movie, music, and game disks in disk storage notebooks or disk organizers. Disks will be protected and easy to find, and you'll never again play "Open the Case" to try to locate the missing copy of *A Christmas Story*.

Tap spaces under shelves and furniture, sliding DVD-filled media boxes underneath end tables. Cable or satellite boxes can live neatly in the space below the entertainment center, if you place their feet on a thin square of plywood to raise them up off the carpet for better air circulation.

Behind the entertainment center, cable wraps or cable organizers keep cables out of sight and safe from children or pets. Be careful to segregate cables when wrapping them; power cables can interfere with signals flowing through audio and video cables, so bundle them separately.

To relieve crowding on family room bookcases, relocate specialty titles to their point of use: cookbooks in the kitchen, idea books in the crafts area, computer books shelved near the computer desk. Assess the surviving books with a critical eye, and put your library on a diet. Reference books and favorite novels make the cut; old school textbooks and dated nonfiction titles can be donated.

Households with children know how quickly a family room can come to resemble a day-care center that's been hit by a hurricane. Building in end-of-day toy pickup routines can help; adding color-coded baskets or stacking bins gives toys a place to congregate without being in the way.

Tuning Your Time-Management Skills

Time … it's the ongoing current on which we float the work of our lives. A truly democratic dimension, time grants each of us the same number of seconds, hours, and days; how we differ is in the way we make use of it.

Whether you want to get more done or to do less and enjoy it more, boosting time-management skills makes the most of this valuable commodity: your time.

In this chapter, we take on calendaring concepts and explore basic routines to keep time on our side. Diving into to-do lists provides practical pathways to reaching goals and getting the job done each day. Finally, we push back against procrastination with a step-by-step plan to break through into productivity.

Boosting Your Calendar Power

To assess your calendar prowess, you first need to know where you stand. A time log makes an instructive exercise, bringing you face to face with the truth about how you manage time.

Create a time log using binder paper, planner pages, or the free printable time log from OrganizedHome.com. In it, conduct an hour-by-hour assessment of what you do each day, noting activities for each waking hour. Using colored markers can help you highlight different activities, such as work, personal care, and household chores.

At the end of the week, you'll have created a visual map of where your time goes each day. You'll be able to see which activities are oversubscribed and which priorities are being shunted aside. A time log clarifies whether you have a realistic grasp on expectations, making overscheduling obvious. Time-gobblers and bad habits will stand out, as will any mismatch between your personal circadian rhythms and your activities. Use the guidance a time log provides to set goals for better management of your time.

Create a Single Calendar

In the conflict between you and the clock, a personal calendar is the first tool in your arsenal. You'll use it to schedule your time and decide when to carry out the work of your life. Make a good start by setting up a personal calendar and using it to outline your day.

Whether entrusted to a computer, a paper daily planner, or free printable schedules from OrganizedHome.com, your calendar acts as a map of your time. Use it to allocate your day into activity segments: to work on goals, handle the business of life, or engage in social activities. Reviewing the calendar provides feedback about where you need to fine-tune your use of time.

Personal preference will dictate the complexity of your daily calendar. Do you prefer to group activities into several broad categories, blocking out time for each? Then a simple daily schedule may be enough to keep you on track. More complicated lives that juggle competing work, household, and community commitments may need to plan time in hourly increments or smaller.

Calendar format is also an individual decision. Those who live life attached to the terminal find it convenient to rely on computer software for time management. Others prefer the simplicity and ease of pen and paper. Review your time log and your goals to decide on a calendar format that's right for you. You'll want power enough to handle everything you'll throw at it, with sufficient simplicity for ease of use.

Basic Routines for Time Management

Calendar in hand, develop a set of simple routines for good time management. Working one at a time, add these new habits to your daily life:

- **Carry your calendar with you always.** Out and about, our lives are filled with decisions about time. Will we need to make an appointment, check availability, or agree to attend an event? It's hard to know what to do when the calendar's somewhere else. Keep your personal calendar close at hand for easy consultation on the go.

- **Depend on it daily.** Add "calendar check" to morning and evening routines. Before bed each night, review what you'll be doing the next day in time to make any night-before preparations. Consult your calendar each morning to refresh your memory on the events ahead and to hit the ground ready to roll.

- **Track deadlines.** Use your daily calendar to remind yourself of upcoming deadlines. Whether you count down with daily assignments or post a reminder of an impending deadline a few days ahead, creating a calendar tracking system will keep you moving forward.

- **Set targets.** To meet goals, work backward. To complete a handmade Christmas gift, for instance, enter benchmarks in your calendar, making entries on the dates you will plan the project, purchase supplies, reach the halfway point, and complete the item. Break down goals backward to plot their trajectory in your calendar.

- **Let your calendar be your naysayer.** Answering requests for your time with an automatic "let me check my calendar and get back to you" avoids the need for an immediate answer and gives you breathing room to evaluate the request privately and honestly.

- **Build in buffer zones.** When estimating time entries on your personal calendar, build in buffer zones. Overstate the time you think you'll need, or create small pockets of free time between one activity and the next. Build in wiggle room for life's inevitable delays and distractions.

- **Trap ideas and reminders.** Do you rely on bits of paper to record phone numbers, appointments, and reminders? To get organized, you need to stop shedding Post-It notes like leaves in autumn. Trap these nuggets of information in your calendar, whether it's a paper planner or a smartphone's dictation function. Create a one-stop home to store these stray bits of information.

Shared and Household Calendars

Where possible, avoid double or multiple calendars. They waste time and lead to scheduling conflicts. Instead, explore ways to create shared calendars that allow for synching and collaboration, without having to resort to segregated scheduling for family, work, and community events.

SPEEDY SOLUTION

Online family organizers make it easy to share calendars with an entire household. With email reminders, smartphone apps, and the ability to sync with computer calendars, free services like Cozi.com and Google Calendar offer fast solutions to coordinate life at home.

Another solution is to set up a calendar on behalf of the entire household. Think of the household calendar as a planner for your home—a centralized list of activities and events. While each family member maintains a personal calendar, the household calendar belongs to the house as a whole.

A household calendar is one case where sticking to a paper format trumps flashier alternatives. Post it in a public place, and no one will need to flip open a phone or boot up the computer to check dates for social engagements or team practices. Household helpers, such as babysitters, can access the calendar's information without needing to sync up in any particular electronic platform.

Use the household calendar to coordinate weekly schedules, family vacations, or church functions. Add chore reminders and family workdays to keep household functions humming. Include birthdays and special occasions so everybody's aware of an upcoming anniversary. Transfer information from school calendars and sports team schedules so the whole household knows who belongs where and when. A well-seasoned household calendar tells everyone who lives there what's going on and what needs to happen in the house that week.

Hold regular family scheduling sessions to keep the household calendar current. Add "calendar check" to weekly routines to keep family members on the same page ... literally!

Crafting To-Do Lists

Calendars establish your schedule, but to make the best use of that time, you'll need to rely on a specialized tool: a set of to-do lists.

To-do lists have three functions. First, they're goal-setting engines that break down a goal and place each step onto the revolving belt of daily life. Second, to-do lists act as an extra lobe of the brain; they supplement your memory by recording all the small stuff you hope to accomplish. Finally, to-do lists track progress; they record your achievements and help you identify breakdowns in movement toward a goal.

Most of all, using to-do lists brings stress relief! Offloading to the to-do list the job of deciding what to do each day lets you take a deep breath and get to work.

To make effective use of to-do lists, start and keep a master to-do list, a running list to record everything from broad goals to one-off minutia. From the master to-do list, you'll generate daily to-do lists to guide each day's activities and ensure that items don't drop off your radar if left undone.

The Master To-Do List

Think of the master to-do list as a dumping zone—and a collection bucket for personal goals. It's the place where you write down all the little must-do, should-do, want-to-do ideas that cross your mind, along with the big "someday, I'd like to ..." goals that lie close to your heart. By relocating these entries from your thoughts onto paper, you'll be ready for the next step: prioritizing them and putting them into action.

In its format, the master to-do list can be as simple as a few sheets of lined paper or as complex as a dedicated goal-management computer program.

To begin a master to-do list, take a few minutes to write down everything—and I do mean everything—that's weighing on your mind at the moment. On your list, you'll see a mix of entries, ranging from broad goals to one-time reminders, such as these:

- I want to learn Spanish.
- I've got to do something about my hair!
- Call the vet to check on Duff's blood work.
- Start planning our summer vacation.
- I need to finish replanting the new flowerbed.

Scribble them down quickly, without regard to order. The important step is to move them from mind to paper. Shifting these items from mind to list stops them from buzzing aimlessly around in your head and gives you a platform for beginning to deal with them.

To build the master to-do list, add entries as they occur to you, or tackle the list during regular planning sessions. The important thing is to generate the list: it's your springboard to action.

The Daily To-Do List

The master to-do list provides raw material for the next step: assigning tasks to a daily to-do list. A running list of things we need to do, the daily to-do list focuses attention on the day ahead and sees to it that we get the job done.

Many people use a free-form list of daily tasks, but most of us will benefit from dividing the daily to-do list into broad action categories. For ease of use, consider subdividing your list into sections like these: To Go, To Do, To Buy, To Call, Follow Up, Decide, and Delegate.

At its simplest, the daily to-do list is just that: a list of things we need to accomplish that day. A daily to-do list keeps us from crashing around in an unproductive fog by keeping us focused on the work of the day.

To create each day's to-do list, check the preceding day's list for unfinished tasks and add them to the current one. Next, review the master to-do list and assign one or more items to the current day's agenda.

Reward yourself by crossing items off your list as soon as you complete them. Seeing a visible reminder of your progress creates a sense of accomplishment.

The Supercharged To-Do List

Making and using to-do lists goes a long way toward getting a grip on mundane chores, but what do you do about entries like "I want to learn Spanish"? You supercharge the to-do list productivity tools by using them to break down broad goals into smaller steps and bringing those steps to action.

You start with the master to-do list, looking for entries that represent goals, not chores. Assign each larger goal a fresh section further down the list, with space to break down the goal into manageable steps.

To plan a vacation, you'll need to set a budget, research locations, check in with family members, arrange time off, and make reservations, so list each of these steps. Since they're sequential (you can't make reservations until you decide where and when to go), add suggested completion dates to your list. By breaking the job into smaller steps, you're ready to feed it to the daily to-do list, one action at a time.

Broader goals, such as learning to speak Spanish, may require you to break down the project two or more times before you can separate out individual action steps. Known as "chunking," this process subdivides a large goal into manageable chunks of related actions, making it easier to convert the goal to specific, listable actions.

Finally, use your master to-do list to set priorities for competing projects. While a visit to Spain (and speaking the lingo like a native) is a long-cherished dream, it may need to take a back seat to other goals, such as completing the training you need to apply for a promotion. Even if it's not at the top of your priorities, your master to-do list will safeguard those "someday" goals until it's their time to shine.

A Procrastinator's ABCs

Procrastination is the enemy of good time management, and most of us suffer from it to a greater or lesser degree. It causes us to stall out, delay, or dawdle when taking on a job we know we have to do. Getting past procrastination is a core skill for good time management.

Whether you suffer from it as a passing malaise or a chronic condition, get procrastination out of your way by remembering the procrastinator's ABCs: take **a**ction, **b**reak it down, and **c**reate momentum.

Take Action

Since procrastination holds us in a state of suspension, simply making a start can break through it as easily as a footstep shatters an icy puddle. Taking one step forward, no matter how small, releases the energy that was keeping you imprisoned and static. Try these tactics to take that all-important first step:

- **Start small.** If you're truly dreading the task, bite off the tiniest chunk possible to begin. Getting over it and getting started can calm the anxiety and get you underway with the rest of the job.

- **Do the worst first.** Jump-start action by beginning with the toughest, most dreaded segment of the task. By getting the worst of it out of the way, you'll make the rest of the chore look easy by comparison.

- **Reward yourself.** Reduce resistance to a dreaded job by offering yourself a carrot, not a stick. Before you begin, brew a favorite beverage and put on music that motivates you. Associate the postponed task with pleasant circumstances, to create motivation to dive in and get it done.

- **Beat the clock.** Trick yourself into taking action by
  scheduling the job immediately before something else
  you'd like to do. Take on the task a few minutes before
  a favorite television show begins, and try to see how
  quickly you can carry it out. Focusing on speed, not the
  task at hand, short-circuits the inner procrastinator.

Break It Down

Procrastination can surface when the task you're avoiding feels
overwhelming or poorly defined. The solution is to break the job
into smaller steps so that you can see the way ahead clearly.

Removing any confusion about how to proceed sidesteps procrastination in favor of taking action. By focusing on one step at a
time, breaking down the job shifts mental energy and undercuts
the desire to put off the whole thing.

Create Momentum

When fighting procrastination, you can make a start and break
it down, but with some jobs, you just can't lose that heavy feeling
of "I don't want to!" If this variant of procrastination dogs you
every step of the way, try this tactic: create momentum.

As you carry out the job, whenever you need to take a break,
don't do it at the end of a step! Doing so just brings procrastination back to bear when you must pick up the next piece of the
process.

Instead, pick a stopping point right in the middle of an action.
When you return to work, your next step forward will be obvious, sitting there right in front of you. The momentum you've
created will carry you past the temptation to put off the task one
more time.

Conquering Household Paperwork

It's inevitable: into each day, some paper will fall. Do you have an efficient system for handling the business of your household?

To stay on top of paperwork and keep home finances humming, a home office activity center provides space and storage for handling household business efficiently. In this chapter, you'll learn basic paper-handling routines and a three-part household filing system to help you process the paperwork and get it where it needs to go, fast. Finally, we'll take aim on paper piles with quick ideas to cut them down to size.

Creating a Home Office Center

Where do you go when it's time to get down to the business of life? If you're paying bills at the kitchen table and piling paperwork in odd corners, it's time to find your center. Take care of the business end of your organized life by setting up a home office to handle scheduling, bill paying, correspondence, and mailing chores.

This specialized activity center can be located in a single room, should you be so lucky, but it can also live in a spare corner or even inside a closet. As you work, you'll appreciate peace and quiet, so choose a low-traffic location in the home. The space you select should be large enough to hold a desk, a computer workstation, files, and supplies.

Next, consider the roster of activities you'll carry out in your home office activity center. Paying bills and filing household information are core activities in a home office; scheduling, communications, correspondence, and mailing are allied functions. You may want to combine command central—your life-management center—with the home office area for an all-in-one planning solution.

At the heart of the home office lies the desk, the surface that will hold your work. When setting up a workspace, take personal filing preferences into account. Filers, who work well with information tidied away, need less desk space than pilers, who are most comfortable when they can spread things out. Computer users need space for peripherals such as printers and scanners.

Consider comfort and ergonomics when you select a home office chair. Since you'll spend considerable time in it, look for a model with appropriate back support and adjustable height.

Climb the walls to keep information in view but off the desk. Bulletin boards, whiteboards, or wall-mounted paperwork organizers keep your desk clear and ready for action. Yes, you'll want to add decorative touches to the home office, but confine photos and artwork to the walls, where they will inspire you without getting in your way on the work surfaces.

Finally, make space for filing. Whether you use a file drawer contained in a desk, a rolling file cart, or a piler-friendly desktop combination of in and out boxes and a tabletop file holder, you'll need easy access to your most important paperwork.

Establishing Financial Routines

Managing money can be something of a juggling act. A good juggler keeps all the balls in the air easily, sending each of them around their orbit with a small push at the right time. Drop one ball, however, and the whole act bounces to a halt until you can retrieve the balls and set them in motion once again.

It's the same way with managing household finances. Filing receipts and paycheck stubs on a regular basis means you know where they are when tax season arrives. But if you shove stacks of paper into odd corners month after month, expect to spend days playing hunt-down-the-statements when April 15 rolls around. The secret to staying organized with your finances is in the routines: small, regularly scheduled sessions that maintain momentum in your financial life cycles.

Establishing simple routines for mail handling, bill paying, and filing cuts the time and trouble it takes to manage household finances. Your accountant, not to mention your spouse, will thank you if you keep up with the business of your life on a regular basis.

Mail and Paper Handling

Each day, sort the mail as it arrives. At the trash and recycling area, dump catalogs you don't want, magazines you don't read, and junk mail you didn't request straight into the recycling bin, reserving only unsolicited credit card offers. These will need to be shredded to prevent identity theft, so they require further action.

If you still receive physical copies of bills and credit card statements, open the envelopes and divest them of their clutter of promotional inserts and extra pages. Save space in your files by retaining only the statement itself and the return envelope.

Sort remaining business mail straight into a set of action files, depending on whether you need to pay, respond, file, or decide what to do about each item. Finally, pass along personal mail for other household members, adding it to their launch pad or personal action file folder so they know where to find it and can retrieve it.

SPEEDY SOLUTION

Use a letter opener to skim open letters, bills, and bank statements. An old-school tool that's still sharp, a letter opener opens envelopes quickly and cleanly without damaging the contents.

Bill Paying and Financial Management

In the old days, when bills were delivered by snail mail and banks took several days to process paper checks, paying bills once or twice a month was a possibility. In today's fast-paced, electronic climate, haphazard bill paying is a surefire way to rack up late payment charges and trigger interest rate increases.

Decide how frequently you will check your finances and pay bills. A weekly routine should keep you on top of money matters; if you do your banking online, it may be more comfortable to check bank balances and scheduled payments daily. Either way, add a bill-paying session to daily or weekly routines to keep the financial pipeline flowing freely.

To make it easy to remember who must be paid when, rely on a page-at-a-glance record of monthly household bills. Write out a list of bills on a sheet of paper or the free printable bill tracker from OrganizedHome.com, or set up a list in your financial-management software program. For each item, note due dates and payment amounts.

Automate your financial life with electronic bill pay. It offers 24-hour convenience and cuts the costs of postage and paper checks. If you're not yet paying bills online, add one or two new payments to your bank's online portal each month. Within a year, you'll have made the transition to paperless without much effort.

Once online, make bill paying automatic whenever possible. Setting up regular, scheduled payments heads off late payment fees and makes it easier to set up a budget. For bills with a variable amount, estimate a ballpark figure for what you'll owe each month and schedule payments anyway. Tweak each month's payment amount as bills arrive.

 ROAD HAZARD

Paying bills and handling banking online is wickedly convenient, but internet transactions can and do go wrong. Bookmark banking websites and check them regularly, or use a smartphone app to keep close tabs on automated accounts. Head off problems at the pass, not after the money has flown!

Filing

For many folks, filing paperwork ranks right up there with dental work in the "I don't want to!" category of dreaded activities. Nobody disputes the value of a well-maintained set of files, but no one except the most extreme filers enjoys the process of creating one.

Take the trouble out of the task by setting up a simple, dynamic trio of household files that will automatically shunt paper from arrival to action, and from reference to retention (an organized household filing system is outlined in the next section). Then build your filing speed and prowess with some quick tricks to short-circuit the process and turf piled-up papers quickly.

Setting Up Household Filing Systems

Make it easy to keep household and financial paper flowing to the place where it belongs by setting up a three-part filing system to route paperwork. *Action files* provide short-term storage for items when action is needed; *basic files* offer ongoing reference to items when action has been concluded. Finally, *classic files* retain information you need in the long term. Together, these filing systems create a three-step conduit to prevent paper pileups and keep information flowing freely.

Action Files

When papers enter your home, each one requires an action, even something as swift and final as sending a credit card offer to the shredder. That's why the first phase of an organized household filing system is the action file: a small set of files for incoming documents, grouped according to action.

Action files represent the intake step of the paper-filing process. Without regard to category, and without giving them a permanent home, action files nudge each slip of paper into the chute according to what type of decision or action you'll need to take next with it.

A simple tabletop file holder is all you need to speed each new piece of paper on its organized way. Grab six to eight file folders or hanging files, and label them according to the action required. Some common action file headings are:

- To Do
- To Pay
- To File
- To Read
- Contacts
- Calendar
- Waiting/Pending
- To Decide

Some action file headings, like "To Do" and "To Pay," are self-explanatory. A questionnaire you must return is a to-do item, while bills and credit card statements live in the "To Pay" folder until it's bill-paying day. Information that you need to retain but that requires no further action goes in "To File," while an article your mother sent you waits in the "To Read" folder until you have time to check it out. If your doctor has moved to a new office building, toss the announcement into the "Contacts" file, and add a save-the-date card for an upcoming family wedding to "Calendar."

Watch out for the "Waiting/Pending" file. This folder exists to hold completed items that are waiting for a response, such as copies of a pending product rebate. When the rebate check arrives, it'll be safe to toss the paperwork—but until that date, give it a home in the "Waiting" file, in case you need to follow up on a missing rebate.

By contrast, the "To Decide" folder holds items about which you need to make a decision. An invitation to a fundraiser you're not sure you want to attend is a "To Decide" item. Keep this distinction in mind—use the "Waiting/Pending" folder when you expect a further response from others; use "To Decide" if you need to respond to something and need time to ponder what you yourself would like to do.

Once a week, sit down with the action file and clear it out. Pay bills, update the calendar, and check up on items in the "Waiting/Pending" folder; then send each item of paper to its next station: your set of basic files.

 ROAD HAZARD

With credit card fraud rampant, set aside an action file just for receipts and dump them daily. When statements arrive, tick off the receipts against the bill to help you spot any fraudulent charges. Toss the small stuff, but retain receipts for big-ticket items, in case of returns or warranty work.

Basic Files

Basic files are closer to what we think of when we hear the words *filing system*. Separating bills, information, insurance policies, and correspondence into categories, basic files are home to papers that need no further action but that have to hang around for information's sake.

To create basic files, start by establishing a few broad divisions that make sense to you. Big-picture categories such as paid bills, financial documents, reference material, and household information are typical categories for a basic file. Color-code file folders by category to point you in the right direction quickly.

Within each category, you will need to subcategorize as well. For example, a "financial" category might include separate file folders for bank statements, investment records, receipts, and tax documents. Household information might be subdivided into folders for product warranties, health records, pet records, and service agreements.

Overly complicated filing systems can be frustrating to use, so combine subcategories wherever you can. For example, file all credit card statements in a single "Credit Cards" folder; a folder labeled "Communication" can hold bills for landline phone, cable television, and internet service providers.

Play to your individual filing preference as you set up basic files. If you're a filer, you'll be more comfortable making filing divisions at a greater depth. People with piling tendencies see their comfort zone satisfied with larger, less complex groupings. Your goal is to be able to file and find any item quickly, but the level of complexity you need to do so will depend on your comfort level.

Store basic files within arm's reach of your home office workstation. As you empty action files weekly, deposit each completed item straight into the appropriate basic file. To keep weekly filing simple, and because you may need to refer to items filed there, keep basic files stored close to your work area.

Classic Files

Classic files are the resting place for items that you must retain for a period of time but that you don't expect to need. Income tax returns, paperwork related to a mortgage or car loan, and correspondence files with friends or loved ones should live out the remainder of their useful lives in classic files.

Classic file categories typically mirror the broad divisions of basic files, and duplicating the basic file setup makes it easy to graduate older items from basic to classic. You'll stock classic files once or twice a year, generally at tax time, or at the conclusion of major transactions. As you sort statements or gather documents for the taxman, transfer older items to their corresponding classic file.

Classic files can be stored away from the home office, as long as they're placed in a spot that will allow access with reasonable effort. Labeled records boxes work well to safeguard classic files, and stack and store easily.

ROAD HAZARD

Standardized lists of what paperwork to keep, and how long to keep it, are a lot like one-size-fits-all pantyhose: they don't fit any individual person very well. Check with financial advisers to come up with a custom retention schedule for your household to be sure you're keeping only those documents you really need.

Quick Tricks to Conquer the Paper Pileup

When tackling household paperwork, try these ideas to speed filing and finding information in your organized home:

- **File daily.** Keep "to file" items from piling up and cramping your style and your filing area by filing daily. Send mail to action files as you sort it; tuck completed

items straight into their basic folder after you pay or
review them.

- **Clean out files yearly.** Spring cleaning isn't just for
  walls and windows. Tax season is a great time to clean
  out files, shredding items you no longer need to keep.

- **Firm up a filing position.** Do you file papers to the
  front of each folder so the newest ones show up first, or
  do you prefer to file to the back so documents arrange
  themselves chronologically? Both methods have their
  partisans, but consistency is more important. Pick a
  filing position, and then stick to it to avoid confusion
  and the rearranging of papers.

- **Tab to the front.** If you place tabs on hanging file
  folders on the front edge of the file, you'll always be
  able to see them. Placed on the back edge, papers stored
  inside the file can obscure the tabs, making them harder
  to read.

- **Junk the junk mail.** Cut down on paper clutter by
  putting a stop to unwanted catalogs and promotional
  mailings. To opt out of catalogs quickly, check online;
  many companies provide a simple form for subscription
  removal. Removing your name from a list takes just a
  few seconds.

- **Banish the filing backlog.** Getting organized in
  an ideal world, we'd start fresh with new filing and
  paperwork systems. The reality is, many of us have
  large stacks of neglected papers to cope with. To nibble
  the stacks down in record time, attack the job in tiny
  increments, such as every day during a commercial
  break in a favorite television program. Review, toss, and
  file just 10 to 20 items in short breaks to keep forward
  momentum flowing.

Getting Organized in the Workplace

>> **In This Chapter**

- Coexisting with other organizing styles
- Clearing clutter in your work area
- Organizing office spaces efficiently
- Managing time at work

Getting organized at the office is a lot like getting organized at home. You'll use many of the same tools and techniques, and face many of the same challenges. However, the presence of co-workers and the demands of corporate culture may impose some constraints when you reach for your organizing solutions. Working within those limits and creating routines ideally suited for office activities will bring more time and productivity to your workday.

In this chapter, we discuss ways to work in harmony with people or places with divergent organizational styles. We take a look at ways to cut office clutter and how best to organize your workspace for success. Finally, we examine helpful routines and checkpoints that will speed and organize your working life.

Surviving an Alien Organizing Style

At home, most of us have some experience dealing with differences in organizing style between ourselves and other family members. Even though styles may clash and tempers flare, messy folks and neat freaks can and do learn to exist more or less happily together.

In an office setting, striking a balance between different organizing styles can be a bit more difficult. Someone who likes to tackle complex chores first thing in the morning, and work without interruptions until noon, may be stymied by an office culture that makes a ritual of midmorning meetings. Pilers may feel pressure to adopt more rigid filing habits; filers may not find office-sanctioned filing systems sufficiently trustworthy to handle their information. Anyone on either extreme of the clutter tolerance spectrum, whether it's working in stark space or cozy clutter, may run afoul of informal office norms about the appearance of workplace space.

Try these ideas to harmonize your work life with your individual preferences. Resolving conflicts where you can, and learning to work around those you can't, is a threshold skill for staying productive on the job.

Time Management

Get a good idea of where you need to improve time management by creating a time log, tracking what you do each hour for a full week. Identifying what the problems are and understanding why they're occurring is the first step to being able to resolve them.

Accept the guidance your time log will bestow. For some, internal time rhythms don't sync neatly with established office hours. Early birds fare better if they handle routine matters in the afternoon so that they can maximize their most productive hours early in the day. By contrast, if you find morning hours hard going, slot the low-bandwidth tasks before lunch, and take on the tough stuff when your energies surge in the afternoon.

If your day is fatally fragmented by interruptions and meetings, making it hard to complete projects, shifting your work hours earlier or later may help you wall off the uninterrupted time you need. Consider establishing "unavailable" periods during the day, blocking out time in your schedule and sending phone calls to voicemail for the duration.

Space Allocation

Working with others means sharing office space—and files, equipment, and supplies, too. To do so happily, compromise is the name of the game. Look for creative ways to walk to your own organizational beat in the midst of workplace chaos.

In shared workspaces, take control of your personal work zone where possible by setting boundaries. Erecting real or virtual barriers between your desk and the rest of the world lets you set up an organizing microclimate that better suits your needs. Rely on bookcases or cubicle walls to set the boundaries of your space, and then arrange your stuff and storage according to your own preferences.

Solutions as simple as facing away from the door when working can discourage incursions when they're not welcome. Headphones wall off sound and send a signal to others that you're engaged elsewhere.

Clutter Variances

Working with others who don't share your general level of clutter tolerance can be frustrating. A supervisor of the clean-freak persuasion looks askance at your cozy cubicle, or the doting auntie at the next desk has covered half the nearby shared wall space with photos of various nieces and nephews. How do you negotiate a happy medium?

If you're bothered by other people's clutter, find ways to wall it off from your vision as you work. A row of books supported by bookends at the end of the desk, or a shift of your desk orientation may take the distracting images out of your field of vision.

To find common ground with someone who has less clutter tolerance than you do, look for ways to contain your clutter for a neater appearance. Relocating piles to a stacking set of desk trays will keep things in view where you want them but send a signal of "tidy, tidy, tidy!" to the pile-averse supervisor or co-workers around you.

Controlling Workplace Clutter

Workplace clutter comes in many forms. Documents are dumped on the desk multiple times a day. Email messages surge into the inbox minute by minute. Handouts and presentation tools pile up in corners of the office, while briefcases fill up with swag from conventions and clients.

Tackle workplace clutter with the same tools you use at home. Clear it out regularly, and put safeguards in place to keep it from piling up around your office.

On the Desk

Daily clutter control can keep the level of chaos in an office down to a dull roar. Before leaving each day, clear spaces, file papers, and return office supplies to their proper places.

Once a week, hold a brief STOP clutter session to clear a single drawer, shelf, or file section of clutter. Sort, toss, organize, and put away items to create clutter-free spaces. Over time, your efforts will reduce existing piles and keep new ones from forming.

Don't go overboard on desktop equipment. Keeping more supplies on hand than you can use in the short term eats into valuable desktop space and clutters your work area. Leave the extras in the supply closet or desk drawers to keep desk areas lean, mean, and productive.

Subdivide office drawers with drawer dividers or organizers created for flatware and cutlery. You'll save time sifting through small items to locate a binder clip or staple remover.

Resist the urge to print. While making paper copies can lead to a feeling of security, the practice can also lead to a lot of clutter. Use the printer sparingly to keep from drowning in unnecessary printed items.

After each project is completed, clear the decks. Toss draft copies of documents and tuck away related computer files in an appropriate location. Remove research materials from the desk to create a clean slate for the next project.

SPEEDY SOLUTION

Don't bother keeping hard copies of product manuals and software guides; these reference works are easily available online if you need them.

In Your Space

To cut office clutter, round up the usual suspects: those items that make the transition to clutter right away and don't belong in an organized space. Prime targets include promotional giveaways or convention freebies, superseded drafts of documents or presentations, dried-out pens, and outdated technology items such as floppy disks or low-density thumb drives.

Changing work patterns, such as moving to paperless systems, can lead to a surfeit of unused supplies. Get rid of any office supplies that you haven't used in a year, taking particular aim at outdated technology. If file transfers are now handled online, there's no need to hold on to multiple spindles of burnable CD discs.

Managing Data Clutter

Virtual workspaces, like physical ones, can become cluttered with unneeded items, making the good stuff hard to find. Keep your computer's desktop as spare and organized as you keep the desk where you sit. You'll focus on the day's work more easily if you reduce the number of distracting desktop icons and store project files in document folders.

For most people, email is the primary source of data clutter at the office. To keep junk mail from clogging your inbox, activate spam filters in your mail client to send Nigerian check-cashing scams straight to the recycling bin.

It can be a bit trickier to cut down on "friend spam": those waves of forwarded jokes and links to funny videos that pile up in the inbox. Nicely asking the principal offenders to remove you from their distribution list sometimes works; another way to cope is to send all mail from these sources directly to a subfolder, out of your way.

Just as you clean your desk area, tidy up computer files at the completion of each project. Delete draft versions and consolidate computer files in a single folder. Empty the recycling bin (or trashcan, for Mac users) regularly to purge the hard drive of discarded files.

Organizing Office Spaces

Setting up an efficient office, you'll use the same tools you use to get organized at home, only on a smaller scale.

Visualizing office space as a set of overlapping activity centers helps you locate tools for maximum efficiency. Assigning equipment to storage zones according to use keeps your space workable. Keeping clutter at bay and setting up clutter-containment areas prevents stuff from overwhelming a small workspace.

Making Your Office Work for You

When setting up an office, consider desk placement first. Are you more comfortable facing the door or pointed away from passing distractions? Locate your chair at a spot that energizes you, and then build your desk around you.

Where standard desks are one-sided, the most functional workspaces are L- or U-shape. If your desk is one-sided, add an attachment, or set a small table or filing cabinet at right angles to the desk and use it to expand your workspace.

Look high and low to find extra storage space in your work area. A computer hutch atop the desk keeps manuals, folders, and reference books close at hand. You can sometimes find extra storage beneath the desk as well; it's possible to store software or supplies on the small shelf found in many desk kneehole spaces.

 ROAD HAZARD

An overload of framed photos and sentimental items can cramp small workspaces. Limit family photos or mementos to one or two special items, and hang them on the wall to free up valuable desk space. Keep extras in a box and rotate them to keep the display fresh.

Divide your desk area into storage zones according to how easy they are to reach. Shelves and drawers within arm's reach should be kept free of all but essential items. Lower drawers and higher shelves, which can be reached with some effort, make a good place to store the stuff you need less often. Finally, storage space that requires you to move away from your desk, like an office closet, is the proper place to keep extra supplies and equipment you don't use often.

Filing space at your desk is at a premium; reserve that real estate for current projects or for reference material that you consult frequently. Make a home for stale files or lesser-used general reference material away from the desk, or even outside the office, to keep your focus where it belongs.

If you use a paper planner, keep it open and turned to the current day on your desktop. Use it to track to-do items, to record sudden bright ideas, or to note a need to follow up.

The Organized Computer

Your computer is your most valuable office tool, so keep it running smoothly. Keep antivirus and security software current, and download antivirus updates promptly. To keep your computer working well, allow software applications to check automatically for program updates, and install them as needed.

Computer equipment is sensitive to dust and vibration; when possible, avoid storing a computer's CPU unit on the floor where it will be jostled with every passing footstep. Don't install a computer tower in a closed cabinet without ventilation, as heat causes extra wear on processors and circuit boards.

Even the most robust computer search feature can have a hard time finding specific computer files, if you've forgotten where you put them or what you named them. Set up folders in your documents area in categories similar to those you use for physical filing. Organize by project, by vendor, or by client, to keep relevant information together and easy to find.

Develop file naming conventions to organize your computer files, and use them consistently. Solutions such as 2012_01_Collins_Proposal, which specify year, month, and client in the file name, make it easy to sort and locate computer files.

Also develop the habit of replacing spaces in file names with the underscore character (_). Some mail clients, web browsers, and operating systems choke when they encounter empty spaces in file names; others fill them with substitute character strings that can make file names hard to read.

Office Routines and Time Management

The same time- and task-management tools that you've used to organize life at home can also bring your workday under control. Routines, checklists, and to-do lists help you cut through the confusion and make the most of your time each day.

At the office, maintain master and daily to-do lists just as you do in your personal life. A two-step list system organizes the work you need to do and makes sure you get the most important things done first.

Regular "brain dumps" onto a master to-do list cut stress by bringing ideas out of the recesses of your mind and onto paper, where you can address them and act upon them. Use the master to-do list to break down large goals into individual steps. Each day, move items from the master to-do list to a shorter list of daily actions. At the end of the day, shift any undone tasks onto the next day's to-do list so they won't fall between the cracks and not get done.

Streamline paper handling with an office action file. Keep a small desktop file holder to separate incoming paperwork according to whether it's something you need to do, buy, decide, file, delegate, or hold for further information. Adapt the action file principle to your computer inbox as well, to streamline incoming email and triage incoming requests to folders organized according to action.

SPEEDY SOLUTION

Along with a to-do list, consider building a "to don't" list: a short reminder of things that interfere with your productivity. Surfing social networking sites, sending personal email, and asking a certain chatty co-worker about her health are all worthy "to don't" list entries for the office.

Building a Workaday Routine

Developing an office routine is the surest way to get down to work, quickly and well. Bundling a set of steps into an orderly progression, routines speed the job and prevent wasted time.

Begin and end each workday with short routines designed to mark the transitions between work and personal time. Drop car keys in a ceramic dish, hang your jacket, and stow your purse or briefcase as you sit down at the desk; the routine will be the signal to start your day. At day's end, tidy up the desktop, water the office plant, and turn out the lights to tell yourself it's time to leave the office and return home.

Use chunking to carve out specified times each day to answer phone calls, return email, or provide feedback on a needed project. Establishing a set time to receive incoming calls can help keep you from being interrupted throughout the day, so include this information each time you must leave someone else a phone message.

Creating Calendar Checkpoints

Use calendar checkpoints to keep your work life and workspace organized. A few simple routines tied to each day, week, and season keep your organized office in good shape.

The inbox fills up daily, and a bulging inbox is distracting and disheartening. Get in the habit of clearing your inbox at the end of every day. Route email items to action folders in your mail client to keep you focused. If you can do an item in two minutes or less, do it now.

Begin and end each week with a clean slate and clear desk. At the beginning of the week, set the stage for success by arranging materials you'll need for current projects. Before leaving for the weekend, dump clutter, take out the trash, and clear your desktop for a new week.

To stay organized throughout the year, schedule regular office retooling days. Every few months, set aside a day to dive into your workspace, cleaning out files, reorganizing drawers, sorting reading materials, and removing clutter.

Handling Bumps in the Road

As I've said before, getting organized is a journey, not a destination. Nothing underscores this truth faster than watching things fall apart around you under the stress of special circumstances. Family members pushing back against proposed changes in the household, or life events like moving and the holiday season, can leave chaos in their wake.

It's all but inevitable that your newly organized life will be thrown for a loop from time to time. This chapter explores how to include family members in your efforts, cope with life's special challenges, and make your way back from trying times.

Get Family Members on Board

Usually, one family member must lead the way when it comes time to get organized at home. Seldom does everyone in the household realize the need for change at the same moment—and it's even less likely that the whole family will have the same level of motivation. Following are things you can do to encourage family members to join in and get organized with you.

Set the Standard

Remember that change begins with you. To move your household toward a new and organized life, you'll need to set the standard yourself. Get your own act together before you ask for change from others.

By working on personal goals first, you'll bring the benefit of personal experience to the table when it's time to involve the family. With firsthand knowledge of the stresses and successes on the road to change, you'll be better able to craft household-wide solutions that will work for everyone.

Setting a good example inspires and empowers others. If family members see the benefits of the changes you've already made, they'll be more willing to take on new ways of living to continue the trend. The rewards you've reaped can motivate other family members to join you on the organizing bandwagon.

Finally, making a good start for yourself before asking the household to join you heads off those demoralizing fits-and-starts organizing cycles. Nothing immunizes family members against change more than having each get-organized effort fizzle out shortly after it's imposed! When *you* commit to the process first, you'll be prepared to follow through when it's time to bring the family on board.

Consult, Don't Confront

When you're defending hard-won changes in the household's routines, it's easy to come across like a drill sergeant when faced with a resistant family. As tempting as it is to call a whole-house meeting and lay down the law, try to resist the urge to be confrontational. Instead, claim the role of organizational consultant.

As a consultant, focus on helping family members identify problems and create solutions. If there's something in it for them, they will be much more likely to cooperate—and when their own concerns take center stage, motivation is right behind.

Consultants listen as much as they speak; their goal is to draw both issues and answers from the client. In a family, too, you'll reap much more investment in proposed changes when you actively solicit input from others. Don't tell, just ask! Keeping an open mind can lead to solutions where you least expect them.

ROAD HAZARD

Family members may share your house, but that doesn't mean they'll share your unique organizing style. Stay sensitive to differences in clutter tolerance, filing style, and time sense when crafting household organizing solutions. There's no such thing as "one size fits all."

Establish Household Routines

Just as choreography keeps dancers moving in unison, household routines help family members live together in an organized way. By spelling out necessary tasks and setting the sequence for carrying them out, household routines make expectations clear and reduce confusion and conflict.

For example, telling a youngster "Go clean your room!" becomes an exercise in frustration when neither parent nor child agrees on what constitutes "clean." Establishing a list of specific clean-your-room chores—stack stuffed animals on the bed, carry dirty clothes to the laundry area—puts all parties on notice of the standard and the steps necessary to meet it. With a routine in place, everyone understands what needs to be done and when he or she needs to do it.

Use a problem-solution approach when establishing household routines, tackling them one issue at a time. Whether it's getting out the door on time in the morning or tidying up the family room at night, work with family members to develop a short list of tasks that will solve the problem. Focus on carrying out the new routine until it has become a normal part of family life, and then move on to the next challenge.

Also bolster accountability by documenting routines and posting them publicly. Chore checklists and children's star charts make the routine's steps clear while keeping your voice out of the enforcement picture.

Finally, reinforce new routines by pairing them with a reward. An arrangement as simple as "Once all the toys are picked up, it will be time for a story!" goes a long way to sweeten the nightly request to clear the family room floor.

Get Organized for a Move

An old saying says it best: "Two moves equal one fire." Few life events short of a fire create as much domestic disruption as moving your household. When faced with a move, it's easy to feel as if your brain has taken wings and flown away—and it's even easier to lose your organized way on the road to a new home.

You will need to fight back! A well-organized move can mean the difference between hitting the ground running in your new location and taking months to settle in, unpack, and feel at home. Try these ideas to streamline your next move.

Create a Move Planner

An event as complicated as a move—whether across the street or across the country—requires its own command center. Putting a dedicated move planner into play can make the difference between moving madness and a robust relocation.

Choose your favorite format for your move planner—a three-ring binder, paper planner, or electronic organizer. Your goal is to have all information related to the move in one single, portable package.

At the outset, a move planner needs to incorporate time-management basics: a calendar and master and daily to-do lists specific to the move. Your move planner should remind you of what you need to do and when you need to do it—at a glance.

Having contact information handy is critical during a move, so provide a place for it. Whether you use electronic contact management or tuck business cards into a plastic organizer page, make it easy to stay in touch with all the new best friends you're going to be making along the way.

Moving generates paper, so make provision for it as well. You'll want to designate a receipts envelope to corral information for use at tax time. Page protectors safeguard and sort housing applications, repair estimates, and financial paperwork, so add a handful to your move planner.

While moving, keep your move planner with you always. It'll track notes from meetings and phone calls, record house-hunting impressions, and keep the myriad must-do tasks before your eyes. Don't leave home without it!

SPEEDY SOLUTION

To decorate a new home, tuck décor items like paint chips, fabric swatches, and flooring samples into the pockets of clear organizer pages made for baseball cards. When shopping for window treatments, you'll know at a glance whether a given fabric will work with walls and carpet.

Label Everything

Moving is hard enough work as it is, and it's even harder if you have to shift through a whole stack of boxes to locate the ones holding the sheets and pillowcases. The simple solution to this problem is self-adhesive labels.

Before you begin packing for a move, make a trip to the office-supply store to stock up on standard address labels. They're cheap and easy to print, and save immense amounts of time during the packing and unpacking processes.

Before packing begins, print or write on two or three sheets of self-adhesive labels each room or area in your home. Include rooms like "kitchen" and "master bedroom," and add areas like "linen closet" and "storage."

As you pack, slap an appropriate label on each side of every box. Yes, I said four labels per box! Labeling each side provides instant identification of the contents, no matter how the boxes are stacked and jumbled during the move.

At your new home, post simple signs in each room or area of the house to help labeled boxes reach their new location quickly. This will help your movers get your stuff to the right place the first time.

Pack Me Last

Moving day can be so chaotic that the center of a three-ring circus seems peaceful in comparison. Here's a method to make moving day simpler, easier, and more organized: the moving-day box.

As you pack, hold back items that will be needed during the first day or two after you move. For example, the vacuum cleaner, a tool kit, and cleaning supplies will be among the first items you'll reach for in your new home, so pack them last so they're off the truck as soon as you are.

If children live in the household, set aside a television, a DVD player, and a selection of favorite videos to be accessible right away. It will make it easy to entertain them while you work.

Finally, think past moving day to the first night in your new home. For a good night's sleep, make sure boxes containing bed linens, blankets, and an alarm clock are among the last boxes in the van. The next morning, will you need the comfort of your favorite coffee mug? Add a box of breakfast basics to welcome the new day on a happy note.

ROAD HAZARD

Don't pay to transport old clutter to a new home! Keep clutter off the van by routing it out and sending it on its way before you begin to pack.

Plan Holidays and Celebrations

Around the year the calendar turns, bringing with it birthdays, holidays, and seasonal celebrations. Happy as they are, these special occasions can derail even the most organized life. Buying gifts, cooking holiday meals, and entertaining have a cost in time and energy—and organization.

To take the chaos out of festive occasions, advance planning really pays off. Plan your way to smooth celebrations around the year with these ideas.

Set Up a Holiday Planner

The command center concept works just as well to organize holiday celebrations, birthdays, or family gatherings as it does to organize everyday life. Set up a designated holiday planner, or add a "holiday planning" section to your life-management center or daily planner.

In it, include a calendar of birthdays, anniversaries and occasions, gift lists and gift ideas, decoration inventories, and ideas for family traditions. Page protectors can hold recipes, decoration inspirations, and gift suggestions, while a receipts envelope makes gift returns easy.

Break It Down and Begin Early

Each December, the holiday season brings a long list of to-dos, along with decorations. Sure, it's tempting to wait until the spirit moves you to begin preparing for the holidays, but down that path lies grumpy late-night sessions spent wrapping gifts or addressing holiday letters.

To cut the crazy out of Christmas, come up with a plan that breaks down preparations into simple, smaller steps, and then tackle the tasks over several weeks before the season begins. Spreading out the work keeps the joy in the job by preventing seasonal overload and frantic last-minute spending.

When you wait until the last minute to get ready for Christmas, you're apt to turn to credit cards to finance the festivities. Making a gift list and shopping ahead helps spread the financial burden over several weeks, and makes it easier to stick to cash, not credit. Begin early, because consumer debt is nobody's idea of a good holiday gift!

Stockpile Gifts and Greetings

Birthdays and anniversaries come once a year, every year—but too many of us celebrate them with a last-minute dash to the shopping mall. Take the pressure off these special occasions by buying and stockpiling gifts throughout the year.

By thinking of loved ones well before their birthdays or anniversaries arrive, you'll have a chance to find that special, thoughtful gift, without all the last-minute pressure. Maintaining a household supply of suitable gifts for weddings, birthdays, and anniversaries means no last-minute stress when the happy day rolls around. You can simply shop in your own, already-paid-for stockpile.

A small dresser drawer or large shoebox makes an efficient greeting card file for birthday cards, thank-you notes, and condolence cards. Store cards on edge, and use index cards or file folders to divide cards into groups like "birthday" and "sympathy." Stock up on suitable greeting cards once or twice a year. When you need one, flip through the file to find a suitable sentiment.

SPEEDY SOLUTION

Whenever a friend or family member celebrates a birthday, buy their holiday gift at the same time you buy their birthday present. Because you're focused on one loved one at a time, it's easier to find meaningful gifts—and, come December, your budget will thank you!

Last-Minute Company

The phone call begins innocuously: "Hello dear, we're in the neighborhood and thought we'd come by for a visit!" Looking around the house, your heart sinks at the gulf between everyday comfort and company ready.

What's the solution for sudden drop-in visitors? A crisis-cleaning plan. This short list of most important chores gets you ready for guests as quickly as possible—and without spinning your wheels. Whether you have 10 minutes or a whole hour, receive your guests into an organized home with this crisis-cleaning checklist:

If you have 10 minutes:

- Grab a box or bag and remove clutter from the family room or living room. Stow the box in a nearby closet for later retrieval.
- In the kitchen, do a quick clear of kitchen counters. Pop dirty dishes into the dishwasher or stack them neatly in the sink.
- Check the dining table. Sweep clutter aside, collect newspapers or mail, and straighten placemats and table decorations.
- Close doors to bedrooms or bathrooms guests won't visit.

If you have 30 minutes, add these tasks:

- Make a quick swipe of the guest bathroom. Swab the sink, toilet seat, and under the toilet rim. Put out a fresh hand towel for guest use.
- Light a scented candle or give your home a quick spritz with scented room spray.
- Make space in the coat closet for guests' coats and belongings.

If you have an hour, also include:

- Vacuum the family room, kitchen, and entryway.
- Dust family room furniture.

Reclaim Your Organized Life

Life happens, and sometimes it has a way of burying our best efforts to stay organized. For a variety of reasons, all of us find ourselves back at square one from time to time.

How do you climb back out of the hole? By revamping your life-management center, getting a quick grip on creeping clutter, and learning from your mistakes to stay organized for the long haul.

Revamp Your Control Center

Just as your control center serves as a focal point for getting organized in the first place, so, too, will it help you dig out of a hole. Thankfully, you can restart your control center easily and simply whenever need be.

To jump-start your control center, start with your calendar and update it. Comb the stacks and piles on the desk, and check bulletin boards for notes concerning upcoming appointments, events, and commitments. Enter them all into your calendar and move on.

Next, update planning pages. Turn to the master to-do list, and check it to see that it's up-to-date. If life has slid too far, start a new master to-do list, transferring any undone items.

Finally, begin a new daily to-do list. Checking the revitalized master to-do list, set aside the day's "To Do," "To Call," "To Go," and "To Buy" entries. Whether you use electronic list management or a simple paper planner, jump-start the days ahead with a freshly formatted daily to-do list.

 ROAD HAZARD

Faced with a meltdown of new organized habits, it's easy to become discouraged and give up altogether. Stop right there! Just as you don't let one missed class keep you from the gym forever, keep the tone in your organizing muscle by getting back on track as quickly as possible.

Corral Creeping Clutter

Clutter is persistent and sneaky. The minute your back is turned to deal with a new personal or life crisis, it's easy for clutter to sneak back in the door and take up residence again.

Thankfully, it's also easy to send creeping clutter on its way. Just as you did when you cleared clutter the first time, use the STOP clutter method to quickly eliminate clutter enclaves. Using the four boxes marked "Donate," "Store," "Throw Away," and "Give Away," move to each area of clutter to sort, toss, organize, and put away until you've restored your organized space.

Focus on clearing counters first; then move on to clutter in living areas. Finally, tackle any clutter that's washed up in closets, cupboards, and drawers. If there is an organized base beneath the new layer of clutter, it will be easy to reclaim your surroundings.

Learn from Your Mistakes

Each time your organized life falls apart, take a look at the underlying causes. What you'll learn will help you avoid the potholes in the future, and bolster your organizational skills.

To learn from your mistakes, answer the following questions. Record the answers in your command center planner for future reference. They'll guide you to a more organized life in the future.

1. What exactly went wrong? Did clutter get a foot in the door and propagate around the house again? Did an illness or a busy stint at work lead to a collapse of household routines? You'll need to understand the cause to keep the problem from happening again.

2. What were the danger signs? What did you notice first: creeping clutter, time-management meltdown, or disorganized spaces? Identifying the first signs of an organization breakdown will help you spot it earlier next time and take action.

3. What was the effect of the disorganization? If you understand what went missing when life fell apart, you'll place more value on your efforts to stay the course.

4. What could you have done differently? Write down solutions that might have worked so that you can implement them the next time life goes off the rails.

Organizing Resources

To get organized fast, find more information, support, and tools for organized living with the resources in this appendix.

Support Groups

Support groups offer day-to-day assistance and a wealth of experience. Speed your journey with these get-organized support groups:

Alt.Recovery/Clutter
groups.google.com/group/alt.recovery.clutter

This is an online mailing list for people recovering from clutter.

Clutterers Anonymous
clutterersanonymous.net

Based on the 12-step method, these groups focus on the underlying causes of clutter.

Messies Anonymous
messies.com

Author Sandra Felton offers daily coaching tips and an online support group for clutterers.

Junk Mail Removal

Cut down on catalogs, junk mail, and unwanted phone solicitations with these resources:

Catalog Choice
catalogchoice.org

Control catalogs that you receive with this free opt-out service.

DMA Choice
dmachoice.org

This free service helps you opt out of direct mail (junk mail).

DoNotCall.gov
donotcall.gov

Opt out of phone solicitations at this government website.

Birthday Reminders

These free online reminder services track birthdays and special occasions:

Birthday Alarm
birthdayalarm.com

BirthdayPal.com
birthdaypal.com

HappyBirthday.com
happybirthday.com

Online Selling and Trading

Try these online sites to sell or trade unneeded items:

eBay
ebay.com

This is an online auction site for all kinds of items.

Paperback Swap
paperbackswap.com

Trade paperbacks online at this site.

Play It Again Sports
playitagainsports.com

Locate consignment stores for sports equipment.

Online Family Organizers

Keep your family life on track with helpful tools:

AboutOne
aboutone.com

This site provides a household-management service with integrated smartphone apps.

Cozi
cozi.com

At this site, you'll find a full-featured family calendar and organizer.

FamJama
famjama.com

This is a free online family scheduling service.

10-Step Organizing Plan

The fastest way to get organized is to focus on your own challenges, strengths, and goals. Use this quick step-by-step organizing plan to create a custom path to your organized life:

1. To get off to a good start, tackle one nagging organizational issue that affects you on a daily basis. This early success will motivate you to make more positive changes along the way.

2. Review the core four components of an organized life discussed in Chapter 1. Which component represents your biggest challenge? Rank the remaining three components in order from weakest to strongest, and then tackle your personalized plan in that order.

3. Review Chapter 2 and note your level of clutter tolerance; decide whether you're a filer, a piler, or a denier; and take note of your time-management preferences. These personal parameters will guide your goals as you address disorganization.

4. Set up a control center—a life-management center for planning, time management, and paper handling. Stock your control central with the tools and supplies you'll need.

5. Begin working on the core component that represents your biggest challenge. If it's clutter, schedule regular STOP clutter sessions and plan a whole-house clear-a-thon. If routines are your weakest point, spend the next

three weeks adopting one new, helpful routine. For disorganized spaces, create one new activity center in a household problem area. If better time management is your top priority, tackle your calendar and to-do lists first.

6. At the three-week point, stop and review your progress. Have your new habits taken hold? If so, move on to the next core component on your list, building on your success. If you need more time to reinforce new routines, commit another three-week period to consolidate your success.

7. Sustain the forward momentum by creating maintenance routines as you reach each goal; they'll help you avoid backsliding while your attention is elsewhere.

8. When you've made substantial strides toward solving your biggest challenge, stop to review your progress.

9. If a special challenge pops up and you get sidetracked, get back on the organized track quickly by jump-starting your control center, making a renewed assault on clutter, and holding a debriefing session to remind yourself what went wrong.

10. Enjoy your organized life!

Index

habits, 49-54
home maintenance, 62
housecleaning, 62-65
laundry, clothing care, 71
menu/meal planning,
  66-69
planning, 54-55
tickler files, 55
time management, 97-98
toy pickup, 94
workplace, 123-124
rummage sales, 29

S

sales, 29
scarcity thinking and clutter
  decisions, 38
seasonal items, 33
seasonal routines, housecleaning, 65
self-coaching, 23
self-sabotage, 19-21
sentiment and clutter decisions, 38
setbacks, 22-23
shared calendars, 98-99
shipping box challenge for
  clutter, 45
single calendar, 96-97
sink activity center, 84
Sort (STOP method), 30
sorting, seasonal items, 33
space optimization
  above cabinet storage,
    79-80
  clutter, 7
  clutter checkpoints, 42-43
  door hangers, 81

multiuse spaces, 82
organized spaces, 7-8
under furniture storage, 79
walls, 80-81
workplace, 117
workplace efficiency,
  120-121
spring cleaning, 65
standard setting with family,
  126-127
starting over, 134-136
starting point, 9-11
STOP clutter method, 28-30
storage, 30
  activity centers, 58
  black holes, 76-77
  containment strategies,
    77-78
  decorations, 75
  door hangers, 81
  entertainment, 93
  food storage, 68-69
  hot zones, 76-77
  kitchen cabinets, above,
    79-80
  location, 75
  online, 47
  options, assessing, 31-32
  planning, 74-75
  remote, bathroom, 91
  seasonal items, 33
  temporary, 32-33
  under furniture, 79
  walls, 80-81
  zone categories, 75
stovetop activity center, 84
style, 13-14
  workplace differences, 116
supercharged to-do list, 102
sweep method for clutter, 31

T

U–V

W–X–Y–Z